UNDERSTANDING Everyday Australian

Book Two

A focus on spoken language
with language reviews, exercises and answers

Susan Boyer

Boyer Educational Resources 2000
Reprinted 2004, 2007, 2008, 2011, 2015

Boyer Educational Resources
PO Box 255, Glenbrook 2773
Phone/fax (02) 47391538

Acknowledgments:
I would like to express my thanks to the following people for their contribution to the final presentation of this book:

Firstly, thank you to Matthew Larwood for his patient consultation regarding the illustrations throughout this book. I would like to say thank you to Jeanette Christian and Alison Hey for their careful proofreading. I am grateful also to teachers at Western Sydney Institute of TAFE who trialed some of the material contained in this book and suggested improvements. I am particularly indebted to the many students who gave me insight into the needs of English language learners, studying in Australia.

I wish to say thank you to Len Boyer, Clinton Bagley and Jeanette Christian for their contribution to the accompanying audio recording. And again I want to thank my husband, Len, for the many hours he spent working on this book. His encouragement and interest has been a tremendous support throughout the project.

Cover illustrations & illustrations throughout this book are by Matthew J Larwood.

Images used herein were obtained from IMSI's MasterClips Collection,
1895 Francisco Blvd. East, San Rafael, CA 94901-5506, USA, and from Microsoft's Clip Gallery Ver 4.0. Microsoft Pty Ltd, 65 Epping Road, North Ryde, NSW, Australia.

The kookaburra clip art was obtained from Australian Graphics Selection, New Horizons, Armidale, Australia.

National Library of Australia
Cataloguing-in-Publication data:

Boyer, Susan
Understanding Everyday Australian - Book Two: a focus on spoken language with language reviews, exercises and answers.

ISBN 978 0 9585395 3 1

1. English language - Spoken English - Australia - Textbooks for foreign speakers.
2. English language - Spoken English - Australia - Problems, exercises, etc. I. Boyer, Leonard, 1951- . II. Title.

428.34 Printed in Australia by Snap Clarence Street, 131 Clarence Street, Sydney 2000

DEAR ENGLISH LANGUAGE STUDENT,

Welcome to ***Understanding Everyday Australian - Book Two.*** This book, along with its accompanying audio recording, has been designed to help you to understand English as it is spoken in everyday situations in Australia. As a student of English as a second language, I am sure you are aware of the difference between the formally presented language of the textbook and the speech you hear, outside the language classroom, in your daily activities and conversations with Australians.

Using this book, along with its accompanying audio cassette, you will discover the meaning of many widely used colloquial expressions. The book also focuses on other aspects of spoken English which are employed by native speakers every day. For example, you will learn expressions used when offering advice, making requests and disagreeing politely. You will also practise listening for important aspects of English pronunciation, such as the use of unstressed syllables and sound linking between words, as well as the different sounds of English.

In some units of this book you are asked to check words in a dictionary, so have a good dictionary nearby while you are studying. Because English words are not always pronounced as they are spelt, you will also need to use a dictionary to learn the correct pronunciation. ***A good dictionary will give clear examples of pronunciation and a pronunciation key***. The Pronunciation Key (usually at the front of the dictionary) will show symbols used for different sounds.

NOTE

Many dictionaries use the same pronunciation symbols as the **PHONEMIC CHART** at the back of this book. However, some dictionaries use different symbols, so it's important to check which symbols ***your*** dictionary uses.

I sincerely hope you enjoy and benefit from using ***Understanding Everyday Australian - Book Two.***

Susan Boyer

ABOUT THIS BOOK

Understanding Everyday Australian - Book Two has been designed so that you can work through it alone, without the help of a teacher, or in a classroom situation with other students. The book contains ten units of work, each based on a conversation about a particular topic. The units are divided into ***six parts*** which have been designed to introduce unfamiliar language, ***step by step,*** in a gradual and systematic way. The layout of the book is as follows:

Part 1 - Focus on listening for general understanding

Part 1 introduces the topic and invites you to listen to an everyday conversation and answer a few general questions by putting a tick next to the correct answers. You will be listening for ***general*** understanding of the conversation only. (You will not need to understand every word). This is an important step as it will help you to realise that it's not always necessary to hear every word to understand the general meaning of a conversation. In some units, you are asked to check words in a dictionary, so have a dictionary nearby when you are studying.

Part 2 - Focus on reading & finding the meaning

In this section, you will ***read*** Conversation 1 as you listen again. When you have finished listening, your task is to ***compare Conversation 1 with Conversation 2*** (which will be next to Conversation 1). Conversation 1 contains the everyday expressions and Conversation 2 contains an interpretation of the expressions in Conversation 1. This section will help you to learn the ***meaning*** of the everyday expressions.

Part 3 - Focus on listening for detail

Now you will listen to Conversation 1 again and write in the missing words in the spaces as you hear them. Don't worry about spelling as this exercise focuses on your ***listening skills***. Listen to the conversation as many times as you like, then check your answers (and spelling) by comparing what you have written with Conversation 1.

Part 4 - Focus on writing for reinforcement

This section reinforces (strengthens) your memory as you listen once more to Conversation 1 and tick the newly learnt everyday expressions on the list as you hear them. Then you are asked to look at the list of expressions (all taken from Conversation 1) and try to remember their meaning. Write in the ones that you can remember, then check your answers by reading Conversation 1 again or checking the reference list at the back of the book. This may seem like hard work but ***writing*** the meanings of the newly learnt expressions is a useful way of reinforcing what you have just heard and read.

Part 5 - Focus on revision

Now it's time to test yourself and see what you have learnt by trying the language review. In this section, you are asked to use the newly learnt expressions in a different context. Firstly, you are asked to complete sentences with an appropriate expression and then complete a crossword. The answers to the crosswords can be found in the back of the book.

Part 6 - Focus on spoken language

This section focuses on other aspects of spoken English which make it difficult for learners to understand native speakers. Each unit highlights and explains a particular aspect of pronunciation, sentence structure or conversation strategy which was used by the speakers in Conversation 1 of that unit. In this section, there will be exercises for you to complete to help you understand, learn and remember.

Language Reviews

After Unit 3, Unit 6 and Unit 10, you will find a language review which consists of the recently introduced expressions and pictures for you to match together. This will help you to see how much you have remembered. Don't worry if you make a mistake - you are still learning.

IMPORTANT NOTE TO STUDENTS

Please be aware that the meaning of colloquial language is ***very dependent on the context or situation in which it is used.*** *'Understanding Everyday Australian'* has been designed to ***introduce and explain*** the meaning of colloquial expressions used by English speakers in the everyday situations presented in this book. However, because colloquial expressions can have different meanings in different situations, it is not advisable that students of Australian English immediately begin using the newly introduced expressions indiscriminately. It would be much better to spend time listening, recognising, and understanding the correct meaning of expressions in different situations ***before you use them*** in your conversations. Therefore, the author and publisher of this book will not be responsible to any person, with regard to the misuse of language, caused directly or indirectly by the information presented in this book.

UNDERSTANDING EVERYDAY AUSTRALIAN - BOOK TWO

CONTENTS

GLOSSARY OF LANGUAGE TERMS

Use this list as a reference while you are using this book.

adjective: a word which describes things, (***black*** car) people, (***beautiful*** girl) places, (***multicultural*** city) or events (***exciting*** race), etc.

article: *'a', 'an', 'the'* are called articles (see page 31 for details)

auxiliary verb: a 'helper' verb which is used with another verb to form tense. (eg. ***will*** come, ***did*** come, ***have*** come) Modal auxiliary verbs are used with another verb to show mode or manner. (eg. ***should*** come, ***might*** come, ***must*** come).

discourse marker*:* a word or expression which shows the speaker's attitude to what is being said. Discourse markers ***show connection*** between what has already been said and what will come next. (eg.'*...however,..*', '*I'm sure you'll agree...*'). See page 45,46.

imperative: base (simple) form of a verb, used at the beginning of a sentence to give orders, instructions, directions. (eg. ***Be*** quiet; ***Turn*** left at the next corner). See page 87.

noun: a word which names **things,** (eg. car, sky); **places** (eg. Australia, ocean) **people** (eg. John, Australians), as well as **abstract things,** things we can't see but can experience/talk about. (eg. history, pain, ideas, education).

pronoun: a word which is used in place of a noun. eg. ***it, she, they***. (See pages 56 & 65.)

verb: a word which shows **action**. eg. He **ran** all the way.
or **state/experience**. eg. She **is** a student; I **have** two children.
Base form can refer to the simple present form of the verb. eg. be, go.

verb tenses: tenses show the **time** of an action, event or condition. Some examples are:

past simple tense: indicates finished past action. eg. He ***went*** to Asia last year. ______ last year ▼ ______ now

present perfect tense: a) used for an action/experience which began in the past and has continued to the present. eg. I **have lived** here since 1998. eg. 1998 ◀——————▶ now

b) used when a past action/experience (which happened at an unspecified time) has present significance. (See page 32) (unspecified time)

eg.. He ***has been*** to Asia. ◀- - - - - - - - -▶ now

present simple tense: a) indicates a present condition/fact.

eg. I ***am*** hungry. eg.

now/present time

b) indicates a present routine. eg. I ***work*** four days each week. eg.

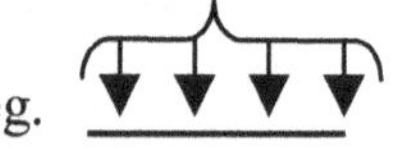

present progressive: (also called present continuous) a verb form made with ***am/are/is +...ing***.
a) This tense is used to talk about an action which is happening at the time of speaking. eg. We ***are waiting*** for him.
b) The present progressive is also used to refer to a future arrangement. eg. He ***is leaving*** tomorrow. For details on future use of this tense see p. 99.

future simple tense: will +verb indicates future time. eg. I think, it ***will rain*** tomorrow. now tomorrow.
See pages 97 to 99 for ways of talking about the future.

NOTE: This list is not intended to be comprehensive. Refer to a comprehensive grammar book for more details.

GLOSSARY OF LANGUAGE TERMS - PRONUNCIATION

Pronunciation practice is an important aspect of language learning and therefore plays an important role in this book. Use this list as a reference as you are using this book. Also see the Phonemic Chart, page 136.

vowel letters: There are **five vowel** ***letters*** in the English alphabet. These are: **a**, **e**, **i**, **o**, **u**.

vowel sounds: There are **twelve vowel** ***sounds*** in English represented by phonemic symbols.

There are seven short sounds: /æ/, /e/, /ɒ/, /ə/, /ʊ/, /ʌ/, /ɪ/,
as well as five long sounds, /ɑː/, /iː/, /ɔː/, /ɜː/, /uː/.

The most frequently used of these vowel sounds is /ə/. This symbol represents an ***unstressed sound***. See page 12, Unit 1 for details.

diphthongs: Diphthong sounds are made from two vowel sounds put together.

There are eight diphthongs: /aɪ/, /aʊ/, /eɪ/, /eə/, /ɪə/, /ʊə/, /əʊ/, /ɔɪ/.
For examples of words containing these sounds see the Phonemic Chart (p. 136).

consonants: The letters in the English alphabet which are not vowels, are called consonants.
These are: **b**, **c**, **d**, **f**, **g**, **h**, **j**, **k**, **l**, **m**, **n**, **p**, **q**, **r**, **s**, **t**, **v**, **w**, **x**, **y**, **z**.
Additional ***consonant sounds*** (represented by the following symbols) are:

/θ/, /ð/, /ʃ/, /tʃ/, /ʒ/, /dʒ/, /ŋ/. Check the phonemic chart (p.136) for examples.

syllable: Spoken words are formed with **syllables**, meaning **sounds**.
A syllable is a unit of unbroken sound, usually containing a vowel sound.

word stress: In words with more than one syllable, one sound is usually stronger (spoken more clearly) than the other(s). The term, ***stressed syllable***, refers to the strongest (primary) sound in words of more than one syllable.

Important Note

A good dictionary will provide very useful information on how to pronounce words correctly. At the beginning of your dictionary, you will find a Pronunciation Key which will show you the symbols used throughout the dictionary to guide you with correct pronunciation.

Many dictionaries use the same pronunciation symbols as the **PHONEMIC CHART** at the back of this book. However, some dictionaries use different symbols, so it's important to check which symbols ***your*** dictionary uses.

If your dictionary does not have a pronunciation key which is easy to understand, you should get a better dictionary.

A good dictionary will also show how ***word stress*** is shown on all words listed in the dictionary. Dictionaries use various symbols to show which syllable should be stressed, so it's important to check which symbol ***your*** dictionary uses.

For example, in the word *open* (which contains two syllables), the stress is on the first syllable. Look at the way this may be shown in a dictionary.

* some dictionaries show a small stress mark **' *before and above*** the stressed syllable. eg. 'open.
* some dictionaries show a small stress mark **' *after and above*** the stressed syllable. eg. o'pen.
* some dictionaries use ***a line under*** the stressed syllable, to show the stressed sound. eg. ***o*** pen

To avoid confusion, always check which symbol ***your*** dictionary uses.

UNIT 1

A TELEPHONE ENQUIRY

You need to let us know ASAP.
Places usually get snapped up as
soon as they become available!

Unit 1 - A TELEPHONE ENQUIRY – Part 1

Using the telephone is a convenient way to get information, however it can be difficult if you are unable to understand fast speech or you are unfamiliar with expressions being used.

Listen to this conversation in which Chris is phoning a college for information about a course he is interested in. The conversation contains colloquial or everyday expressions that will be explained later in the unit - so don't worry if you don't understand every word. This time you are only listening for a general understanding of the topic. As you listen, tick the correct answers below. (There may be more than one correct answer.) When you have finished you can check your answers on page 112.

1) Chris is inquiring about:

a) an Aviation Course.

b) an Office Skills Course.

c) an English Language Course.

2) When did the course start?

a) last week.

b) three days ago.

c) three weeks ago.

3) Chris can't join the class because:

a) it's too late to start.

b) the class is full.

c) the class was cancelled.

4) When do the computing courses start:

a) next week.

b) on Thursday.

c) in three weeks time.

5) Chris decides to:

a) wait till next term before enrolling in a course.

b) enrol in a computing course now.

Now we'll look at the everyday expressions used in the conversation - turn to the next page.

Unit 1 - A TELEPHONE ENQUIRY – Part 2A

CONVERSATION 1 (with everyday expressions)

Read this conversation as you listen to the audio cassette. Do you know what the *underlined* words mean? They are colloquial or 'everyday' expressions.

Receptionist: West Town Institute. Can I help you?

Chris: I'd like to speak to someone about enrolling in the Office Skills course, please.

Receptionist: ***Hold the line*** please. I'll ***put you through***.

Assistant: Office Administration. Can I help you?

Chris: Yes. I'd like to enrol in your Office Skills course for this term, please.

Assistant: Oh, I'm sorry, that course is already ***under way*** for this term. It started last week. I can ***put you down*** for the next course, if you like.

Chris: I'd really like to start now, if I can. Would it still be possible to join this class? I know I'm late but you see, I've only just ***found out*** about it.

Assistant: Well, normally it wouldn't be a problem...as ***a rule of thumb*** students can still join a class in the first week if there are vacancies. The problem is, this course is completely full, I'm sorry. I can ***take your details*** and let you know if any places become available. There's always ***the off chance*** that someone may ***pull out*** during the first week. It happens ***from time to time***.

Chris: OK. Could you tell me when the next course starts, please?

Assistant: Yes, I'll check on the computer...Oh unfortunately, that course is already full too.

Chris: Oh! Well is there a possibility of a second Office Skills course next term?

Assistant: Yes, there's been talk of it but there's some ***red tape*** involved and it's still ***up in the air*** so ***I wouldn't count on it***...Look, I've just noticed there are vacancies in some of our short computer courses starting next week, if that's any help to you.

Chris: That could be ***a goer***. A computing course'd give me ***a head start*** in the Office Skills course later. How much is it?

Assistant: The cost depends on which level you do. I'll send you some information and an enrolment form if you're interested.

Chris: Mm... I ***may as well***.

Assistant: Well, if you definitely want to join the class, you need to let us know ***ASAP***. Places usually get ***snapped up*** as soon as they become available.....and I'm sure you don't want to ***miss the boat*** again!

Chris: That's true...Would it be possible to fax the enrolment form to me? That way I can send it back to you ***this arvo***.

Assistant: Yes, of course. I'll just get your details. What's your fax number............

Now let's see what these expressions mean - look at the next page.

Unit 1 - A TELEPHONE ENQUIRY – Part 2B

CONVERSATION 2 (explanation of everyday expressions)

Compare Conversation 1 with Conversation 2 **-You will see that some of the words are different but the meaning is the same in both conversations. Find the underlined words in Conversation 1, then find the words with the same meaning in Conversation 2.**
For example: *Hold the line.* (Conversation 1) = *Wait a moment.* (Conversation 2)

Receptionist: West Town Institute. Can I help you?
Chris: I'd like to speak to someone about enrolling in the Office Skills course, please.
Receptionist: Wait a moment, please. I'll connect you to the department.
Assistant: Office Administration. Can I help you?
Chris: Yes. I'd like to enrol in your Office Skills course for this term, please.
Assistant: Oh, I'm sorry, that course is already in progress for this term. It started last week. I can write your name on the list for the next course, if you like.
Chris: I'd really like to start now, if I can. Would it still be possible to join this class? I know I'm late but you see, I've only just learnt/heard about it.
Assistant: Well, normally it wouldn't be a problem…as a rule for general guidance students can still join a class in the first week if there are vacancies. The problem is, this course is completely full, I'm sorry. I can record your name and address, etc. and let you know if any places become available. There's always a slight possibility that someone may withdraw/cancel during the first week. It happens sometimes.
Chris: OK. Could you tell me when the next course starts, please?
Assistant: Yes, I'll check on the computer…Oh unfortunately, that course is already full too.
Chris: Oh! Well is there a possibility of a second Office Skills course next term?
Assistant: Yes, there's been talk of it but there're some official rules/procedures involved and it's still undecided so don't expect it/rely on it ...Look, I've just noticed there are vacancies in some of our short computer courses starting next week, if that's any help to you.
Chris: That could be a useful/successful project. A computing course'd give me an advantage in the Office Skills course later. How much is it?
Assistant: The cost depends on which level you do. I'll send you some information and an enrolment form if you're interested.
Chris: Mm… I should. (It's probably a good opportunity).
Assistant: Well, if you definitely want to join the class, you need to let us know as soon as possible. Places usually get taken/accepted quickly as soon as they become available.....and I'm sure you don't want to miss an opportunity again!
Chris: That's true...Would it be possible to fax the enrolment form to me? That way I can send it back to you this afternoon.
Assistant: Yes, of course. I'll just get your details. What's your fax number............

What does the receptionist mean by a.s.a.p?
Fill in the missing words.

You'll need to let us know a.s.a.p
*a*___ *s*______ *a*___ *p*__________

Unit 1 - A TELEPHONE ENQUIRY – Part 3

Listen to the conversation again and fill in the missing words. You may have to listen more than once. (Don't worry about your spelling as this exercise focuses on listening skills - you can check your spelling later.)

Receptionist: West Town Institute. Can I help you?

Chris: I'd like to speak to someone about enrolling in the Office Skills course, please.

Receptionist: ***Hold the*** ________ please. I'll ________ ***you through***.

Assistant: Office Administration. Can I help you?

Chris: Yes. I'd like to enrol in your Office Skills course for this term, please.

Assistant: Oh, I'm sorry, that course is already ________ ***way*** for this term. It started last week. I can ***put you down*** for the next course, if you like.

Chris: I'd really like to start now, if I can. Would it still be possible to join this class? I know I'm late but you see, I've only just ***found*** ________ about it.

Assistant: Well, normally it wouldn't be a problem…as ***a rule of*** ________ students can still join a class in the first week if there are vacancies. The problem is, this course is completely full, I'm sorry. I can ________ ***your details*** and let you know if any places become available. There's always ***the*** ________ ***chance*** that someone may ***pull out*** during the first week. It happens ***from*** ________ ***to time***.

Chris: OK. Could you tell me when the next course starts, please?

Assistant: Yes, I'll check on the computer…Oh unfortunately, that course is already full too.

Chris: Oh! Well is there a possibility of a second Office Skills course next term?

Assistant: Yes, there's been talk of it but there's some ________ ***tape*** involved and it's still ***up in the*** ________ so ***I wouldn't count on it***...Look, I've just noticed there are vacancies in some of our short computer courses starting next week, if that's any help to you.

Chris: That could be ***a goer***. A computing course'd give me ***a*** ________ ***start*** in the Office Skills course later. How much is it?

Assistant: The cost depends on which level you do. I'll send you some information and an enrolment form if you're interested.

Chris: Mm… I ***may as*** ________.

Assistant: Well, if you definitely want to join the class, you need to let us know ***ASAP***. Places usually get ***snapped*** ________ as soon as they become available.....and I'm sure you don't want to ***miss the*** ________ again!

Chris: That's true...Would it be possible to fax the enrolment form to me? That way I can send it back to you ***this arvo***.

Assistant: Yes, of course. I'll just get your details. What's your fax number............

Now check your answers by comparing this page with CONVERSATION 1

Unit 1 - A TELEPHONE ENQUIRY – Part 4

In order to become more familiar with these new everyday expressions:

1) **Listen to Conversation 1 again and tick the boxes ☐ next to the expressions as you hear them.**
2) **After the conversation has finished, write in the definitions you can remember. Some have been done as examples.**
3) **Check your answers by turning to page 126.**

☐ hold the line..............................*wait a moment*...

☐ put (you) through...

☐ under way..

☐ put (you) down ....*write your name on the list*..............................

☐ found out..

☐ a rule of thumb...

☐ take (your) details...

☐ the off chance...

☐ pull out...................................*withdraw/cancel*..

☐ from time to time..

☐ red tape..

☐ up in the air..

☐ *I wouldn't count on it..

☐ a goer...

☐ a head start..

☐ I may as well...*I should do it (It's probably a good opportunity)*.......

☐ *ASAP..

☐ snapped up...

☐ miss the boat...

☐ this arvo...

LANGUAGE NOTES:
The expression, *'I wouldn't ***count on*** it', can also be expressed as 'I wouldn't ***bank on*** it'
or... 'Don't ***count on*** it', can also be expressed as...... 'Don't ***bank on*** it'.
****ASAP*** (as soon as possible) can also be written as ***asap***.

Unit 1 - A TELEPHONE ENQUIRY – Part 5

LANGUAGE REVIEW

Complete the sentences, choosing from the everyday expressions which are listed below. You can use the clues in brackets ( ) at the end of each sentence to help you. Then complete the crossword using the everyday expressions you have written. The first one has been done as an example.

rule of thumb	off chance	up in the air	snapped up	put me down	~~red tape~~
under way	miss the boat	find out	head start	your details	count on

ACROSS

1) There's a lot of ***red tape*** involved when trying to make changes in government. (official rules)
3) As a ______ ___ ________ you should eat some raw fruit and vegetables everyday. (general rule of guidance)
5) You'll have a _____ _____ in the exams, if you start studying early in the course.(advantage)
7) The meeting had been _______ _____ for more than an hour when he arrived. (in progress)
9) I'll have to hurry and get this job application in by the closing date or I'll _____ ____ ______. (lose an opportunity)
11) When did you _____ ____ about John's illness? (learn/hear about)

DOWN

2) You can ____ ___ ______ to work on Saturday and Sunday if you like, as I need the extra money. (write my name on the list)
4) All the good tickets for the concert were ________ ___ weeks ago, so we'll have to sit at the back of the hall. (taken quickly)
6) Write _____ ________ on the form and put it in the box, if you want a chance to win a car. (your name and address etc)
8) I phoned on the ___ ______ that he may be home but he was out as usual.(slight possibility)
10) Susan said she would be early but don't _______ ____ it. She is usually late. (expect/rely on)
12) My travel plans are ____ ___ ______ ______ as my car needs a lot of repairs and I can't afford to repair it. (undecided)

1 r e d * t a p e

Answers, page 112.

Unit 1 - A TELEPHONE ENQUIRY – Part 6

FOCUS ON SPOKEN ENGLISH

A) Telephoning Strategies - Giving a Reason for the Phone Call

When enquiring by phone, it's important to state your reason for the call clearly.
Notice how Chris introduced his call in Conversation 1.

I'd like to speak to someone about enrolling in the Office Skills course, please.
I'd like to enrol in your Office Skills course for this term, please.

Notice the pattern - 'I'd like to + verb

To the receptionist:	I'd like to	***speak*** to someone about enrolling in the Office Skills course, please.
To the assistant:	I'd like to	***enrol*** in your Office Skills course for this term, please.

We can also say, ***I'm interested in*** enroll***ing*** in your Office Administration course, please.

Notice the pattern:

I'm interested in	verb + ***ing***
I'm interested in	enroll***ing*** in your Office Administration course, please.

PRACTICE

Imagine you are phoning a college to enquire about an English course which was advertised in the local newspaper. Complete the following ways you could introduce your call.

I'd like to ______________________________

I'm interested in ______________________________

B) Making Polite Requests

When requesting favours, we can use the pattern: ***'Would it be possible to + verb.....***
Find two examples of this pattern in Conversation 1, page 6. Complete the sentences below.

1) ***Would it still be possible to*** ______________________________

2) ***Would it be possible to*** ______________________________

Notice the pattern:

	verb (present simple)
Would it still be possible to	***join*** this class.

In Conversation 1, Chris used this pattern because he was requesting favours. He was being polite. However, in some situations it would be ***too polite*** and therefore ***inappropriate*** to use, '*Would it be possible to...*'. For example, if a customer is buying a stamp at the post office he does not need to say, *Would it be possible to* buy a stamp? It is ***too*** polite for this situation.

3) Look at the following situations. In which cases do you think it would be ***inappropriate*** (***too polite***) to use '*Would it be possible to...*'. Mark them with a cross, like this ×.
Mark the appropriate situations with a tick ✔. *Answers: page 112.*

a) You want your teenage son to clean his room. (You have already asked him several times.)
b) You want to leave work early tomorrow as you want to attend an important function.
c) You want to change your dental appointment from Monday to Friday.
d) You want to order coffee at a cafe.

Unit 1 - A TELEPHONE ENQUIRY– Part 6

FOCUS ON SPOKEN LANGUAGE - Aspects of Pronunciation

Spoken words are formed with ***syllables*** (or units of sound). As we speak, some syllables are spoken more clearly or strongly than others. These strong sounds are called ***stressed*** syllables. The weaker or softer sounds are called ***unstressed*** syllables. If you are unfamiliar with a language, it is often easy to miss *unstressed* syllables. This may cause problems, not only in pronunciation, but also with grammar and writing. In this unit, you will practise identifying *unstressed* syllables.

C) Unstressed sounds (syllables)

Read and listen to the first few lines of Conversation 1 again, this time noticing the way Chris pronounces the word '***to***' in his first sentence.

Receptionist:	West Town Institute. Can I help you?
Chris:	I'd like ***to*** speak ***to*** someone about enrolling in the Office Skills course, please

You will notice that he uses an unstressed (weak) sound which is shown in the dictionary as the symbol /ə/. It is important to be aware of this sound as it is used extensively in English. Continue to listen to Conversation 1, noting the unstressed forms used, particularly in words such as 'to', 'for', 'as', 'the'. Being aware of this aspect of spoken English will improve your listening and speaking skills considerably.

D) Word Linking in spoken English

When spoken at natural conversational speed, English words are not always heard distinctly, but are often linked together. You will be familiar with the use of *contractions** in which two words are linked to form one word. For example: I would = I'd; you are = you're, she is = she's, etc.
(*For more practice on the use of contractions see *Understanding Everyday Australian - Book One, Unit 1, page 8*).

Linking of consonant sounds between words

Linking also occurs between words when the final consonant sound (b/d/f/g/k/l/m/n/p/s/t/v/z) of a word is the same as the first sound of the following word. (eg. the ***s*** sound in bu***s*** ***s***top is linked) Listen to the receptionist's pronunciation of 'West Town' in line one of Conversation 1. You will see that Wes**t** **T**own is linked together to become Wes(t) **T**own. (The consonant sound is said only once.)

Try ***linking*** these words together by sounding the final and initial consonants only ***once***.

bad dog becomes **ba‿dog** | **night time** becomes **nigh‿time**

top place becomes **to‿place** | **feel lonely** becomes **fee‿lonely**

kiss Sam becomes **ki‿Sam** | **quick kick** becomes **qui‿kick**

FOCUS ON SPOKEN LANGUAGE - Aspects of Pronunciation (continued)

Linking of final consonants and initial vowel sounds

In spoken language we also tend to link the ***final consonant sound*** (b,d,f,g,k,l,m,n,p,s,t,v,z,) of one word to the ***initial vowel sound*** (a,e,i,o,u) of the following word. Look at the following sentences, which have been taken from the introduction of Conversation 1.

> Receptionist: West Tow**n** **I**nstitute. Ca**n** **I** help you?

Now listen to the sentences on your audio-cassette. Can you hear the way the words are linked?

Tow***n*** ***I***nstitute becomes Tow***ni***nstitute

Ca***n*** ***I*** help becomes Ca***nI*** help

Now pronounce these expressions from Conversation 1, by linking the final consonant of the first word with the initial vowel of the next word.

found out	becomes	foun **d**out
pull out	becomes	pu **l**out
up in the air	becomes	u **pi**n the air

> ***REMEMBER***
>
> As 'a rule of thumb', linking occurs between words when:
>
> - the final consonant sound (b/d/f/g/k/l/m/n/p/s/t/v/z) of one word is the same as the first sound of the following word. eg. bu**s** **s**top → bu stop
> - the final consonant sound (b/d/f/g/k/l/m/n/p/s/t/v/z) of one word joins with the initial vowel sound (a/e/i/o/u/) of the following word. eg. loo**k** **o**ut→ loo **k**out

Being aware of this aspect of spoken English will improve your pronunciation considerably.

UNIT 2

TALKING ABOUT STUDY PROBLEMS

Unit 2 -TALKING ABOUT STUDY PROBLEMS – Part 1

Many students don't ask for help with a study problem until it's almost too late to improve their situation. This may be because of embarrassment, laziness or because they don't know that help is available. Have you (or someone you know) ever been in this situation?

Listen to this conversation between friends who are talking about study problems. The conversation contains many colloquial or everyday expressions which will be explained later in the unit - so don't worry if you don't understand every word. This time you are only listening for a general understanding of the topic. As you listen, tick the correct answers below. (There may be more than one correct answer.) When you have finished you can check your answers on page 112.

1) Lynn is worried because:

a) her teacher is sick.
b) she is sick.
c) her teacher is not pleased with her assignment.
d) she may fail her course.

2) She is planning to:

a) go to the doctor.
b) leave the course.
c) go overseas to study.

3) Her friend suggests that she should:

a) transfer to a different course.
b) go on a holiday.
c) ask the teacher how she can improve her assignment.

Now we'll look at the everyday expressions used in the conversation - turn to the next page.

Unit 2 - TALKING ABOUT STUDY PROBLEMS – Part 2A

CONVERSATION 1 (with everyday expressions)

Read this conversation as you listen to the audio tape. Do you know what the *underlined* words mean? They are colloquial or 'everyday' expressions.

Adam: Hi Lynn. How're you going?

Lynn: Oh, not very well, really.

Adam: Why? ***What's up***?

Lynn: Oh, it's this course I'm doing. I'm just ***not keeping up***. I know - it's my fault. In the beginning I was ***too laid-back;*** thinking it would be ***a piece of cake***. I didn't even ***turn up to*** half the classes. Well, I've had ***a rude awakening***. I just received my major assignment back and the teacher said it's ***not up to scratch*** and the way things are looking I'll probably fail.

Adam: So what're you going to do now?

Lynn: I've been thinking about it and I've decided to ***drop out***. It seems I'm ***not cut out for*** this course.

Adam: You can't be serious. You can't ***throw in the towel*** now. Think of all the time you've ***put in***.

Lynn: I know, I've thought of that but I don't think I have much choice.

Adam: Oh, come on. There're other options to just ***giving up***.

Lynn: Like what?

Adam: Well, maybe you could transfer to a course more suited to you.

Lynn: No. I've got ***Buckley's chance*** of getting into another course now – it's too late. Besides, I'd prefer to ***see this course through*** if I'm going to do anything.

Adam: Well in that case, why don't you go and talk to your teacher? Say that you're going to ***knuckle down*** from now on and ask him for ***some pointers*** on how you can improve your assignment.

Lynn: Mm. I could do that. If I really ***get stuck into it,*** I'm sure I could ***catch up*** on the work I've missed. I would like to ***get through*** this course. OK I'll ***give it a go***.

Adam: ***That's more like it***!

If I really get stuck into it, I'm sure I can catch up!

Now let's see what these expressions mean - look at the next page.

Unit 2 - TALKING ABOUT STUDY PROBLEMS – Part 2B

CONVERSATION 2 (explanation of everyday expressions)

Compare Conversation 1 with Conversation 2 **-You will see that some of the words are different but the meaning is the same in both conversations. Find the underlined words in Conversation 1, then underline the words with the same meaning in Conversation 2. For example: *What's up?* (Conversation 1) = *What's the problem?* (Conversation 2)**

Adam: Hi Lynn. How're you going?

Lynn: Oh, not very well, really.

Adam: Why? What's the problem?

Lynn: Oh, it's this course I'm doing. I'm just not progressing at the expected rate. I know - it's my fault. In the beginning I was too relaxed/lazy - thinking it would be an easy task. I didn't even attend half the classes. Well, I've had an unpleasant surprise. I just received my major assignment back and the teacher said it's not good enough/not of an acceptable standard/level and the way things are looking I'll probably fail.

Adam: So what're you going to do now?

Lynn: I've been thinking about it and I've decided to quit/stop participating. It seems I'm not suited to this course.

Adam: You can't be serious. You can't stop trying now. Think of all the time you've invested.

Lynn: I know, I've thought of that but I don't think I have much choice.

Adam: Oh, that's not true. There're other options to just stopping your effort.

Lynn: Like what?

Adam: Well, maybe you could transfer to a course more suited to you.

Lynn: No. I've got little or no chance of getting into another course now - it's too late. Besides, I'd prefer to persist/continue with this course if I'm going to do anything.

Adam: Well in that case, why don't you go and talk to your teacher? Say that you are going to work hard from now on and ask him for some advice on how you can improve your assignment.

Lynn: Mm. I could do that. If I really try/work hard, I'm sure I could reach/achieve the required level on the work I've missed. I would like to pass/complete this course. OK I'll try.

Adam: That's a better idea.

Now to become familiar with the everyday expressions, practise reading CONVERSATION 1 aloud with a partner.

Unit 2 - TALKING ABOUT STUDY PROBLEMS – Part 3

Listen to the conversation again and fill in the missing words. You may have to listen more than once. (Don't worry about your spelling as this exercise focuses on listening skills - you can check your spelling later.)

Adam: Hi Lynn. How're you going?

Lynn: Oh, not very well, really.

Adam: Why? ***What's*** ____?

Lynn: Oh, it's this course I'm doing. I'm just ***not*** ________ ***up.*** I know - it's my fault. In the beginning I was ***too laid-*** ____; thinking it would be ***a piece of*** ________. I didn't even ***turn*** ____ ***to*** half the classes. Well, I've had ***a rude awakening***. I just received my major assignment back and the teacher said it's ***not up to*** ________ and the way things are looking I'll probably fail.

Adam: So what're you going to do now?

Lynn: I've been thinking about it and I've decided to ________ ***out***. It seems I'm ***not*** ________ ***out for*** this course.

Adam: You can't be serious. You can't ________ ***in the towel*** now. Think of all the time you've ***put*** ____.

Lynn: I know, I've thought of that but I don't think I have much choice.

Adam: Oh come on! There're other options to just ***giving*** ____.

Lynn: Like what?

Adam: Well, maybe you could transfer to a course more suited to you.

Lynn: No. I've got ________ ***chance*** of getting into another course now – it's too late. Besides, I'd prefer to ________ ***this course through*** if I'm going to do anything.

Adam: Well in that case, why don't you go and talk to your teacher? Say that you're going to ***knuckle*** ________ from now on and ask him for ***some*** ________ on how you can improve your assignment.

Lynn: Mm. I could do that. If I really ***get*** ________ ***into it,*** I'm sure I could ***catch*** ________ on the work I've missed. I would like to ***get through*** this course. OK I'll ***give it a*** ____.

Adam: ***That's more like it***!

Now check your answers by comparing this page with CONVERSATION 1

Unit 2 - TALKING ABOUT STUDY PROBLEMS – Part 4

In order to become more familiar with these new everyday expressions:

1) **Listen to Conversation 1 again and tick the boxes ☐ next to the expressions as you hear them.**
2) **After the conversation has finished, write in the definitions you can remember. Some have been done for you as examples.**
3) **Check your answers by turning to page 127.**

☐ What's up?...

☐ not keeping up......................*not progressing at the expected rate*........................

☐ *too laid-back..

☐ a piece of cake...

☐ turn up to.............................*attend*..

☐ a rude awakening....................*a truthful and unpleasant surprise*...........................

☐ not up to scratch...

☐ drop out ....

☐ not cut out for..

☐ throw in the towel...

☐ put in ....*(time/work) invested in*......................................

☐ giving up..

☐ Buckley's chance...

☐ *see (something) through.............*persist/continue*...

☐ knuckle down...

☐ some pointers...

☐ get stuck into it...

☐ catch up..............................*reach/achieve the required level*..............................

☐ get through..

☐ give it a go..

☐ That's more like it! ....

LANGUAGE NOTE:
The expression, *__laid-back__* means to be relaxed, but to be ***too*** ***laid-back*** can mean lazy and therefore has a negative meaning .
The expression, ****see (something) through*** means to continue with a project although there are problems. We can also ***see a person through*** meaning to help them in a difficult situation.

Unit 2 - TALKING ABOUT STUDY PROBLEMS – Part 5

LANGUAGE REVIEW

Complete the sentences, choosing from the everyday expressions which are listed below. You can use the clues in brackets ( ) at the end of each sentence to help you. Then complete the crossword using the everyday expressions you have written. The first one has been done as an example.

~~not up to scratch~~	keep up	turn up	get through	piece of cake	
get stuck into it	throw in the towel	pointers	not cut out for	knuckle down	give up

ACROSS

1) I'm sorry, this work is ***not up to scratch***. You'll have to do it again. (not of an acceptable level)
3) I prefer to do outside work. I'm _____ _____ _____ _____ office work. (not suited to)
5) How do you manage to _____ ___ with all your school assignments and work part time too? (progress at the expected rate)
7) If I _____ ______ _____ ___, I'll be finished my work by lunchtime. Then I can meet you for coffee. (work hard at it).
9) The examination was a _______ ___ _____. I didn't have any problems at all. (an easy task)

DOWN

2) The travel agent gave us some _________ on travelling around America. (advice)
4) I failed my driving test last week so I hope I _____ __________ this time. (pass)
6) If you want to learn English quickly, it's important to _____ ___ to every class. (attend)
8) Don't _____ ___ now. You have almost finished. (stop your effort)
10) When the cricket team lost their tenth game, some of the players decided to ______ ___ _____ ________. (quit/ stop participating)
12) If you want to go overseas next year, you'll have to __________ _______ and save some money.(try/work hard)

6 10

1 n o t * u p * t o * s c r a t c h

2 4 3 5 12 7 8 9

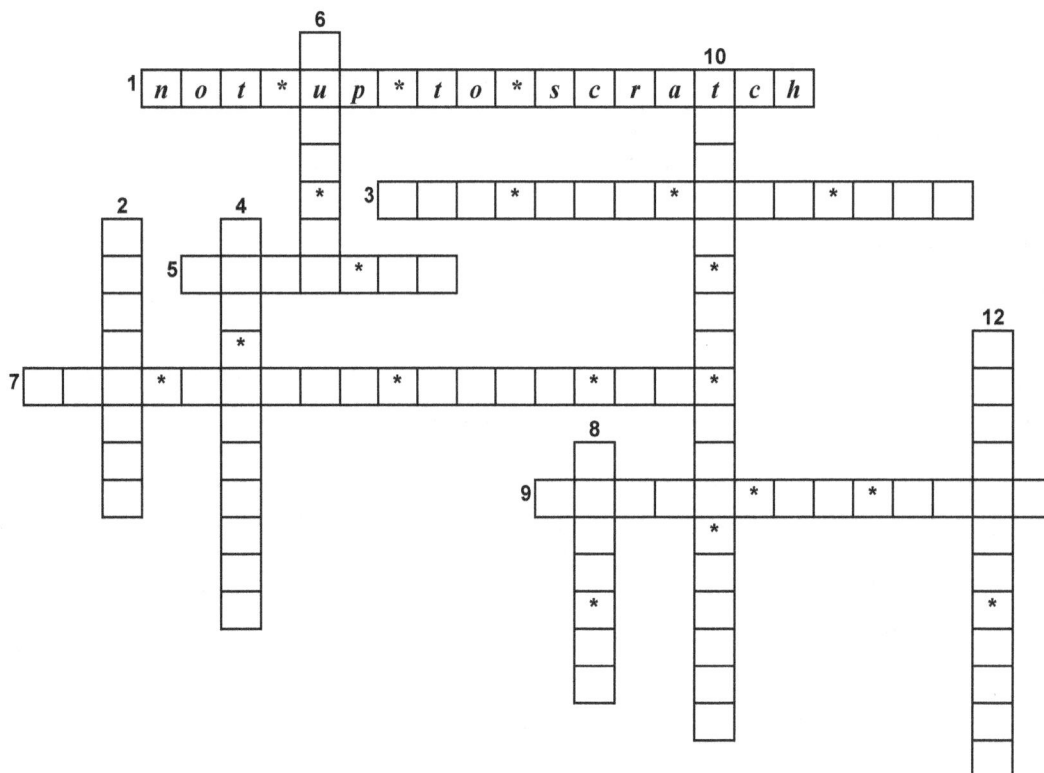

Answers, page 113.

Unit 2 - TALKING ABOUT STUDY PROBLEMS -Part 6

FOCUS ON SPOKEN LANGUAGE

A) Making Suggestions

Listen to Conversation 1 again and notice the expressions Adam used when giving suggestions to his friend. As you listen, complete the following suggestions given by Adam to Lynn.

Suggestion 1) 'Well, ________________________transfer to a course more suited to you'.

Suggestion 2) Well in that case,___________________go and talk to your teacher.'

The following sentences are all different ways of making suggestions or giving advice. Which do you think is the strongest or most direct suggestion? Which is the least direct? Number the suggestions in order of most to least direct. Answers, page 113.

> Why don't you go and talk to your teacher?
>
> You should go and talk to your teacher.
>
> Go and talk to your teacher.
>
> Well, maybe you could go and talk to your teacher.

B) Giving reasons

In Conversation 1, when Adam suggested that Lynn could transfer to a more suitable course, Lynn gave more than one reason for not doing so. Complete the following section from the conversation by writing in the expression Lynn used to introduce her second reason.

'No. I've got ***Buckley's chance*** of getting into another course now – it's too late. __________, I'd prefer to ***see this course through*** if I'm going to do anything'.

'Besides' means *'in addition to this'*, *'also'* or *'as well as this'* and is often used in spoken English to give an additional reason for a decision or action.

For example: 'I don't think I'll go to the club tonight. I'm very tired.
Besides, there's a good movie on TV'.

PRACTICE

In your note book, write several reasons for studying this book. Use 'besides' to add your final reason. (Remember that this expression is mainly used in *spoken* English).

> **LANGUAGE NOTE**
>
> In Conversation 1, when Adam suggested: 'There are other options to just giving up'.
> Lynn replied: ***'Like what?'***
>
> 'Like what?' is an informal expression which means, 'Give me some examples'.
> For example: Lee: 'We'll need to buy some things for the party on Saturday'.
> Kim: 'Like what?'
> Kim's expression **would not** be used **in formal situations** as it could sound too direct.

Unit 2 - TALKING ABOUT STUDY PROBLEMS -Part 6

FOCUS ON SPOKEN LANGUAGE
C) Pronunciation and Spelling

At the back of this book you will find a PHONEMIC CHART to help you identify and practise the various sounds of English.

English pronunciation can be confusing because words are often not pronounced the way they are spelt. For example, in the sentence, 'We are wet', the sound '*e*' in the word '***we***', is different to the sound '*e*' in the word '***wet***'. In the first word, ***we***, '*e*' is pronounced as a long sound, but in the second word, ***wet***, '*e*' has a short sound. In this unit you will practise hearing long and short vowel sounds.

There are only five vowel letters in the English alphabet. These are ***a,e,i,o,u***. However, there are ***more vowel sounds in English than in most other languages***, because each of these vowels can be pronounced as short or long sounds. It is important to be able to hear the difference between short and long vowel sounds.

Pronunciation of vowel sounds /ɪ/ and / i:/

In this unit you will practise identifying and pronouncing the sounds, **/ɪ/** and **/i:/**

/ ɪ/ is a short vowel sound, found in words such as w*i*ll, b*u*sy, p*i*nk, g*y*m, pr*e*tty.
(notice the different ways of spelling the sound /ɪ/).

/i:/ is a long vowel sound, found in words such as gr**ee**n, pl*ea*se, k*ey*, w*e*, s*ei*ze,
(notice the different ways of spelling the sound **/i:/**).

LISTENING PRACTICE

Below is a section from Conversation 1 of this unit. Listen to the conversation again on your audio cassette. Carefully listen to the way the speakers pronounce the words in boxes. Decide which of the sounds in ***bold*** letters are pronounced as a short vowel sound and which have a long vowel sound.

Lynn: In the beg*i*nning I was too laid-back; th*i*nking it would be a p*ie*ce of cake. I d*i*dn't even turn up to half the classes. Well, I've had a rude awakening. I just rec*ei*ved my major assignment back and the teacher said it's not up to scratch and the way th*i*ngs are looking I'll probably fail.
Adam: So what're you going to do now?
Lynn: I've been thinking about it and I've decided to drop out. It s*ee*ms I'm not cut out for this course.
Adam: You can't be serious. You can't throw in the towel now. Th*i*nk of all the time you've put *i*n.
Lynn: I know, I've thought of that but I don't think I have much choice.
Adam: Oh, come on. There're other options to just g*i*ving up.
Lynn: Like what?
Adam: Well, maybe you could transfer to a course more suited to you.
Lynn: No. I've got Buckley's chance of getting into another course now – it's too late. Besides, I'd prefer to see th*i*s course through if I'm going to do anything.
Adam: Well in that case, why don't you go and talk to your t*ea*cher ....

Write the words in the chart on the next page, under the correct symbol. (the first few have been done as examples). When you have finished, check you answers on page 113.

FOCUS ON SPOKEN LANGUAGE - Pronunciation and Spelling (continued)

Words with a short vowel sound /ɪ/	Words with a long vowel sound /i:/
beginning *Thinking*	*piece*

Using a Dictionary Pronunciation Key

Because English words are not always pronounced as they are spelt, you will need to use a good dictionary to show you the correct pronunciation. ***A good dictionary will give clear examples of pronunciation and a pronunciation key***. The Pronunciation Key (usually at the front of the dictionary) will show symbols used for different sounds.

Find the Pronunciation Key in your dictionary now.
If your dictionary is not helpful in showing pronunciation, you should get a better dictionary.

NOTE
Many dictionaries use the same pronunciation symbols as the **PHONEMIC CHART** at the back of this book. However, some dictionaries use different symbols, so it's important to check which symbols ***your*** dictionary uses.
For example, some dictionaries show the long vowel sound in the word *'see'* as **/si:/**
Some dictionaries use a line on top of the vowel to indicate the same sound, see as **/sē/**

To avoid confusion, always check which symbols ***your*** dictionary uses.

PRACTICE

1) Using ***your dictionary*** check the symbol for the short vowel sound in 's**i**t', and the long vowel sound in 's**ea**t'. Copy the symbols from your dictionary onto the lines below.

short vowel sound in **sit** Your dictionary symbol ________ **long** vowel sound in **seat** Your dictionary symbol ________

2) Using ***your dictionary***, check each of the following words.
Do the ***underlined*** vowel sounds have a short or long sound?

English	*seize*	*tea*	*busy*	*pretty*	*key*	*bill*	*magazine*	*big*	*mystery*	*feet*

Write the words in the correct column in the chart below. Then check you answers on page 113.

/ɪ/ **short** vowel sound (eg. sit)	/i:/ **long** vowel sound (eg. seat)

The pronunciation symbols in your dictionary are useful tools for understanding and learning the correct pronunciation of all English words.

UNIT 3

TALKING ABOUT EMPLOYMENT

You need to spell out your abilities and experience so that they stand out.

Unit 3 - TALKING ABOUT EMPLOYMENT - Part 1

(at an employment agency)

Before you listen to the following conversation about employment, match the words in the box with the correct meaning listed below. You can check your answers on page 114.

résumé (also known as CV)	abilities	first aid	qualifications	award wage
relevant	maintenance	supervisor		

skills and talents (things you can do) ____________________________
summary of education and work experience ____________________________
emergency medical treatment ____________________________
training and educational accomplishments ____________________________
the work of keeping things in good condition ____________________________
manager ____________________________
lawfully set guidelines of payment ____________________________
related to the subject receiving attention ____________________________

Now listen to the conversation between Mr White, who is seeking employment, and an employment agent. (Unit 3 on your audio cassette.) The conversation contains colloquial or everyday expressions which will be explained later in the unit – so don't worry if you don't understand every word. This time you are only listening for a general understanding of the topic. As you listen, tick the correct answers below. (There may be more than one correct answer.) When you have finished you can check your answers on page 114.

1) Previously Mr White had worked as:
   a) a travel agent.
   b) a maintenance worker.
   c) an office worker.
   d) a taxi driver.

2) His other skills and qualifications include:
   a) a current driver's licence.
   b) first aid certificate.
   c) a nursing diploma.

3) The employment agent suggests that Mr White should:
   a) improve his résumé.
   b) do a computer course.
   c) write a letter of application.

Now we'll look at the everyday expressions used in the conversation - turn to the next page.

Unit 3 -TALKING ABOUT EMPLOYMENT- Part 2A

(at an employment agency)

CONVERSATION 1 (with everyday expressions)

Read this conversation as you listen to the audio cassette. Do you know what the *underlined* words mean? They are colloquial or 'everyday' expressions.

Interviewer: OK Mr. White, I've ***looked over*** your résumé and I'd like to ***go over*** a few details with you before we proceed any further. I see you've just come back from overseas.

Mr. White: Yes, I was away for about a year on a working holiday. I had a variety of different jobs.

Interviewer: Yes, I see you've written 'handyman' on the form but what did you do specifically?

Mr. White: Well, as I said I had a number of jobs because I was travelling around. I did a bit of maintenance work, ……you know repairing things, painting and some gardening.

Interviewer: I see. Well you need to ***enlarge on*** those skills in your résumé. Don't ***take for granted*** that an employer who reads your résumé will know what you mean by 'handyman'. You need to ***spell out*** your abilities and experience clearly so that they ***stand out***. Remember you need to ***sell yourself***.

Mr. White: Yes, I see what you mean.

Interviewer: OK. Let's take a look at your other qualifications. You have a background in accountancy, data entry and general office duties. Are you hoping to find ***something along the same lines*** again now?

Mr. White: Actually, if possible I'd prefer to ***keep going*** with some sort of outdoor work rather than office work.

Interviewer: Mm. Let's see what we have here. Well…. ***it just so happens*** there is a job available at the hospital for a maintenance supervisor. I ***take it*** you have a current driver's licence?

Mr. White: Yes, and I also have a first aid certificate which I did before I went overseas. I thought it might ***come in handy*** when looking for work.

Interviewer: Good. That's always ***a plus***. Well it looks like you may ***fit the bill*** but you need to bring your résumé ***up to date*** and adapt it to fit this job, highlighting the relevant information ……and you'll need to ***put together*** a letter of application too.

Mr. White: OK. I'll do that this afternoon. Could you tell me what salary I could ***be looking at***?

Interviewer: It depends on experience ***and so on***. I'll check the award and give you ***a rough idea*** of what to expect before I ***set up*** an interview.

Mr. White: OK, that's great. Thanks.

Interviewer: In the meantime, you need to work on your résumé. Oh, and it would be a good idea to ***brush up on*** your first aid too. You may be asked questions about it at the interview.

Mr. White: Good idea! I'm probably a bit ***rusty***.

Now let's see what these expressions mean - look at the next page.

Unit 3 - TALKING ABOUT EMPLOYMENT- Part 2B

(at an employment agency)

CONVERSATION 2 (explanation of everyday expressions)

Compare Conversation 1 with Conversation 2 **-You will see that some of the words are different but the meaning is the same in both conversations. Find the underlined words in Conversation 1, then underline the words with the same meaning in Conversation 2. For example: *looked over* (Conversation 1) = *examined* (Conversation 2)**

Interviewer: OK Mr. White, I've examined your résumé and I'd like to review/discuss a few details with you before we proceed any further. I see you've just come back from overseas.

Mr. White: Yes, I was away for about a year on a working holiday. I had a variety of different jobs.

Interviewer: Yes, I see you've written 'handyman' on the form but what did you do specifically?

Mr. White: Well, as I said I had a number of jobs because I was travelling around. I did a bit of maintenance work, ...you know repairing things, painting and some gardening.

Interviewer: I see. Well you need to explain (those skills) in more detail in your résumé. Don't assume/suppose that an employer who reads your résumé will know what you mean by 'handyman'. You need to explain your abilities and experience clearly so that they are noticeable. Remember you need to promote your value.

Mr. White: Yes, I see what you mean.

Interviewer: OK. Let's take a look at your other qualifications. You have a background in accountancy, data entry and general office duties. Are you hoping to find something similar again now?

Mr. White: Actually, if possible I'd prefer to continue with some sort of outdoor work rather than office work.

Interviewer: Mm. Let's see what we have here. Well.... by chance there is a job available at the hospital for a maintenance supervisor. I suppose you have a current driver's licence?

Mr. White: Yes. and I also have a first aid certificate which I did before I went overseas. I thought it might be useful when looking for work.

Interviewer: Good. That's always an advantage. Well it looks like you may be exactly the right person for the position but you need to change your résumé to include the most recent information and adapt it to fit this job, highlighting the relevant information ......and you'll need to compose a letter of application too.

Mr. White: OK. I'll do that this afternoon. Could you tell me what salary I could expect?

Interviewer: It depends on experience and other things. I'll check the award wage and give you an estimation of what to expect before I arrange an interview.

Mr. White: OK, that's great. Thanks.

Interviewer: In the meantime, you need to work on your résumé. Oh, and it would be a good idea to revise your first aid too. You may be asked questions about it at the interview.

Mr. White: Good idea! I'm probably a bit weak/impaired due to lack of practice.

Unit 3 -TALKING ABOUT EMPLOYMENT - Part 3

Listen to the conversation again and fill in the missing words. You may have to listen more than once. (Don't worry about your spelling as this exercise focuses on listening skills - you can check your spelling later.)

Interviewer: OK Mr. White, I've ________***over*** your résumé and I'd like to ____***over*** a few details with you before we proceed any further. I see you've just come back from overseas.

Mr. White: Yes, I was away for about a year on a working holiday. I had a variety of different jobs.

Interviewer: Yes, I see you've written 'handyman' on the form but what did you do specifically?

Mr. White: Well, as I said I had a number of jobs because I was travelling around. I did a bit of maintenance work, ...you know repairing things, painting and some gardening.

Interviewer: I see. Well you need to ***enlarge***____ those skills in your résumé. Don't ______***for granted*** that an employer who reads your résumé will know what you mean by 'handyman'. You need to _______***out*** your abilities and experience clearly so that they _______***out***. Remember you need to ______***yourself***.

Mr. White: Yes, I see what you mean.

Interviewer: OK. Let's take a look at your other qualifications. You have a background in accountancy, data entry and general office duties. Are you hoping to find ***something along the same***________ again now?

Mr. White: Actually, if possible I'd prefer to ***keep going*** with some sort of outdoor work rather than office work.

Interviewer: Mm. Let's see what we have here. Well.... ***it just so***__________there is a job available at the hospital for a maintenance supervisor. I ***take it*** you have a current driver's licence?

Mr. White: Yes, and I also have a first aid certificate which I did before I went overseas. I thought it might ***come in***_________ when looking for work.

Interviewer: Good. That's always ***a plus***. Well it looks like you may _____***the bill*** but you need to bring your résumé ____***to date*** and adapt it to fit this job, highlighting the relevant information ......and you'll need to _______***together*** a letter of application too.

Mr. White: OK. I'll do that this afternoon. Could you tell me what salary I could ***be***________***at***?

Interviewer: It depends on experience ***and so on***. I'll check the award and give you ***a***_______***idea*** of what to expect before I ***set up*** an interview.

Mr. White: OK, that's great. Thanks.

Interviewer: In the meantime, you need to work on your résumé. Oh, and it would be a good idea to _________***up on*** your first aid too. You may be asked questions about it at the interview

Mr. White: Good idea! I'm probably a bit ________.

Now check your answers by comparing this page with CONVERSATION 1

Unit 3 -TALKING ABOUT EMPLOYMENT- Part 4

In order to become more familiar with these new everyday expressions:

1) **Listen to Conversation 1 again and tick the boxes ☐ next to the expressions as you hear them.**
2) **After the conversation has finished, write in the definitions you can remember. Some have been done for you as examples.**
3) **Check your answers by turning to page 128.**

☐ looked over (something) ....

☐ go over (something)...

☐ enlarge on (something)..

☐ take for granted........................*assume/suppose (something) will be known*...............

☐ spell out...

☐ stand out................................*to be noticeable*..

☐ sell yourself..

☐ something along the same lines...

☐ keep going..

☐ it just so happens......................*by chance*...

☐ take it..................................*suppose*...

☐ come in handy..

☐ a plus..

☐ fit the bill...

☐ (bring) up to date......................*change to include the most recent information/ideas*......

☐ put together...........................*compose*..

☐ be looking at...........................*expect (a certain amount)* ....

☐ and so on..

☐ a rough idea..

☐ set up..

☐ brush up on...

☐ rusty..................................*weak/impaired due to lack of practice* ....

CULTURAL NOTE:

It is appropriate to ask an *employment agent* about salary expectations, as Mr. White did in Conversation 1. However, remember that at a *job interview,* your main aim is to convince your interviewer that you are the best person for the job. So, although it is not inappropriate to ask about salary, do so only after you have promoted yourself and your ability to do the job well. Remember a job interview is your opportunity to 'sell yourself'.

Unit 3 -TALKING ABOUT EMPLOYMENT- Part 5

LANGUAGE REVIEW

Complete the sentences, choosing from the everyday expressions which are listed below. You can use the clues in brackets ( ) at the end of each sentence to help you. Then complete the crossword using the everyday expressions you have written. The first one has been done as an example.

sell yourself along the same lines go over ~~fit the bill~~ a plus stand out enlarged on take for granted spells out brush up on

ACROSS

1) I think I ***fit the bill*** for this nursing job that's advertised in the paper. I have all the qualifications and experience they require. (am the right person for the job)
3) It's important to ______ _________ at a job interview and show that you are the best person for the job. (promote your value and assets)
5) When I finish school, I'd like to do something ________ _____ ______ _______as my brother. He really enjoys his work in advertising. (similar to)
7) My office is very close to the railway station which is __ ______because I don't like driving in peak hour traffic. (an advantage)
9) We'll ___ _____ the plans for our trip again next week, just before we leave (review/discuss)

DOWN

2) My boss always _________ _________exactly how he wants things done so that there are no problems later.(clearly explains)
4) My teacher doesn't _____ _____ _________ that we know what she means. She always checks by asking questions. (assume/suppose)
6) I'll have to ________ ____ ____ my Italian before we go to Rome at the end of the year, as I've promised to be the guide! (revise/review)
8) Today, our teacher _________ ___ the lecture he gave last week. This time I understood everything much better. (explained in more detail)
10) It's a good idea to highlight the most important words in a different colour so they_______ _____ (are noticeable)

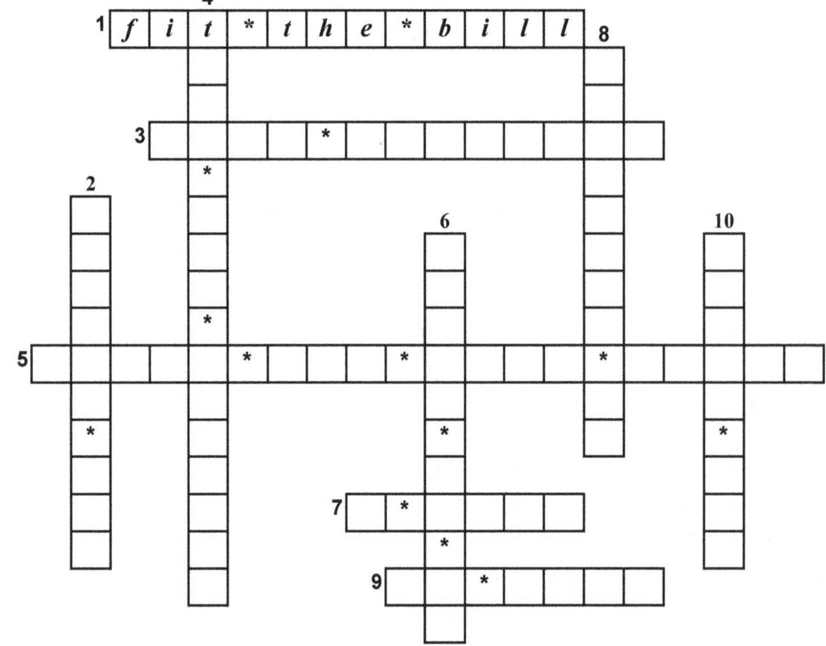

Answers, page 114.

Unit 3 -TALKING ABOUT EMPLOYMENT- Part 6

FOCUS ON SPOKEN LANGUAGE

A) Articles - a, an, the.

Words such as ***a, an, the*** are called ***articles.*** Students of English often have problems knowing when to use articles. This may be because they are usually pronounced as *unstressed* sounds in spoken language and as a result, are difficult to hear. In this unit you will practise listening to the pronunciation of articles and look at the pattern of their use.

How are articles used?
Articles are used before nouns (eg. ***the*** interview) or noun groups (eg. ***a*** working holiday). Look at Conversation 1 again (page 26) and highlight the articles (a, an, the) in different colours so that you can analyse the different ways they are used.

- ***a/an*** are called ***indefinite articles*** because they are used:

a) when we are ***not definite*** (specific) about *which* thing, place, time or person.
   eg. I was away for about ***a*** year on ***a*** working holiday.
b) when we talk about something for the first time in our conversation.
   eg. I have ***a*** first aid certificate. I'll set up ***an*** interview.
c) before expressions of quantity. eg. I'd like to go over ***a*** few details.

The following examples have been taken from Conversation 1 of this unit.

article	*thing (noun or noun group)*
a	few details
a	year
a	working holiday
a	variety of different jobs
a	good idea

article	*thing (noun)*
an	employer
an	interview

Note: ***an*** is used before vowel sounds.

- ***the*** is called the ***definite article*** because it is used:

a) when it is clear from the context *which* thing the speakers are taking about.
   eg. I see you've written handyman on ***the*** form.
b) when we talk about *definite* (specific) things. eg. There's a job available at ***the*** hospital.
c) when we talk about things which have been mentioned previously in the conversation.
   eg. You may be asked questions about your qualifications at ***the*** interview.

Look at the pattern. The following examples have been taken from Conversation 1 of this unit.

article	*thing (noun)*	*reason for using the definite article*
the	form	It is clear from the context *which* 'form' the speaker is talking about.
the	hospital	As there is usually one main hospital in a town, 'the hospital' is specific.
the	interview	The 'interview' has been mentioned previously in the conversation.

- ***No article*** is used when generalising. eg Water is essential for life. (not *the* water or *the* life.)
  I love music. (not *the* music)
  I'm looking for work. (not *the* work)

B) Pronunciation - Listening Practice

Listen to Conversation 1 again and note the *unstressed* pronunciation of the articles, ***a an, the***.

Note: When ***'the'*** comes before a word with an initial vowel sound, as in *'the interview'* at the end of Conversation 1, ***'the'*** is usually pronounced with a long vowel sound, /***i:***/.

Unit 3 -TALKING ABOUT EMPLOYMENT - Part 6

FOCUS ON SPOKEN LANGUAGE

C) Talking about the past (using present perfect and simple past tenses).

In spoken (and written) language we indicate time (past, present, future) through ***verb tenses****.

In Conversation 1 of this unit, a variety of tenses has been used by the speakers. Let's see how the ***present perfect*** and ***simple past tense*** are used in the conversation to talk about the past. Look at this example:

> Interviewer: ....I see you***'ve*** just ***come back*** from overseas.
> Mr. White: Yes, I ***was*** away for about a year on a working holiday. I ***had*** a variety of different jobs.
> Interviewer: Yes, I see that you'***ve written*** 'handyman' on the form but what ***did*** you ***do*** specifically?
> Mr. White: ...I ***had*** a number of jobs.....I ***did*** a bit of maintenance work...

Look at the pattern:

Interviewer's comments, introduced with ***present perfect tense***	Mr. White's reply, using ***past simple tenses***
I see you'***ve*** just ***come back*** from overseas. (*'ve = have*)	Yes, I ***was*** away for about a year.
I see that you'***ve written*** 'handyman' on the form.....	I ***had*** a number of jobs... I ***did*** a bit of maintenance work...

The present perfect tense consists of ***have (or has)+ past participle***.** eg. ***have come, have written***.

- In spoken language, contracted forms are used. (eg. you***'ve*** come; you'***ve*** written; she***'s*** been)
- We use the ***present perfect tense*** to show a connection between the past and the present; to show that the past action/event is relevant at the time of speaking. We usually *don't give a specific time* when the past event/action occurred. eg. 'I***'ve been*** to Europe.'
- We use the ***past simple tense*** to talk about completed events/actions; often saying *when* the event happened. eg. 'I ***went*** to Europe *last year*.'

To introduce a topic about the past in a general way (not referring to specific time) we use the ***present perfect tense***, then continue to talk about it, giving more detail, using the ***simple past tense.***

PRACTICE

The following questions and answers may be heard at a job interview. Complete the questions and answers, adding suitable present perfect and past simple tenses. Answers, page 114.

present perfect tense	***past simple tense***
Have you ***completed*** your training yet?	Yes, I my course in 1997.......
you ***used*** this computer program before?	No, I another program in my last job.
you in a shoe factory before?	Yes, I in a big shoe factory in Taiwan.
you this type of machine before?	Yes, I ***operated*** one like this in my last job.

*** See Unit 7, Part 6 A (page 77) for other ways of talking about the past.**
**** Past participles can be formed by adding '*ed*' to a verb (eg. work → worked) or the spelling may change completely (eg. go → been). See page 124 for a list of irregular past participles.**

Unit 3 - TALKING ABOUT EMPLOYMENT- Part 6

FOCUS ON SPOKEN LANGUAGE

D) Giving informative answers at an interview

At the beginning of Conversation 1, while discussing Mr. White's résumé, the interviewer said, ***'I see you've just come back from overseas'.*** This was a request for more information.

Listen to Conversation 1 again (page 26) and notice that, rather than simply answering 'Yes', Mr. White gave an informative answer, ***'Yes, I was away for about a year on a working holiday. I had a variety of jobs.'***

Also, later in the interview, when the interviewer said, ***'I take it you have a current driver's licence?'***, Mr. White again gave an informative reply, giving more details about himself, rather than just saying, 'Yes'.

Look at the pattern:

Request for information		*Informative reply:*
I see you	***'ve** just* ***come back*** from overseas.	Yes, I was away for about a year on a working holiday. I had a variety of jobs.
I take it you	****have*** a current driver's licence.	Yes, and I also have a first aid certificate which I did before I went overseas. I thought it may come in handy when looking for work

When someone uses the expressions, ***'I see you + verb ....'*** or ***'I take it you + verb ....'*** they are often seeking more details about the topic of conversation.

REMEMBER
An interview presents a good opportunity to give more details on your experience, skills and qualifications so be prepared to give informative answers, rather than simple 'yes'/'no' replies.

PRACTICE

Imagine you are at a job interview. An interviewer is looking at your resume and asking questions. Look at the questions below and give informative answers.

Interviewer: I see from your résumé that you have been studying English?

You: ____

Interviewer: I see you've had some experience doing the same type of work in the past?

You: ____

LANGUAGE NOTE - *the verb 'have'
The verb ***'have'*** is used in a variety of ways in English. See Unit 10, Part 6C (p.109) for details.

LANGUAGE REVIEW ONE

(Units 1 - 3)

This section reviews some of the expressions that were introduced in Units 1, 2, and 3 and gives you a chance to see what you have remembered.

Look at the pictures on the opposite page and decide what the people are saying by choosing from the expressions below.

Match each picture with an appropriate expression by writing the correct letter in the box next to each expression.

For extra practice, you could write the appropriate expression in the space provided in the picture.

1) 'I'm brushing up on the geography of Asia.' ☐

2) 'Could you enlarge on your plans for this area, please.' ☐

3)'This work is not up to scratch.' ☐

4) 'I wouldn't count on getting the washing dry today.' ☐

5) 'We've got Buckley's chance of getting a parking place here!' ☐

6) 'Take this. It'll come in handy if it rains.' ☐

7) 'I'm sorry. You've missed the boat. It's already been sold.' ☐

8) 'I'm not cut out for all this exercise.' ☐

9) 'I'd like something along the same lines as this one.' ☐

(Answers: page 115)

A
T-SHIR
$20
B
PRINCIPAL
C
FOR SALE
D
E
F
COUNCIL
MEETING
G
P
H
I

UNIT 4

TECHNOLOGY AND BUSINESS

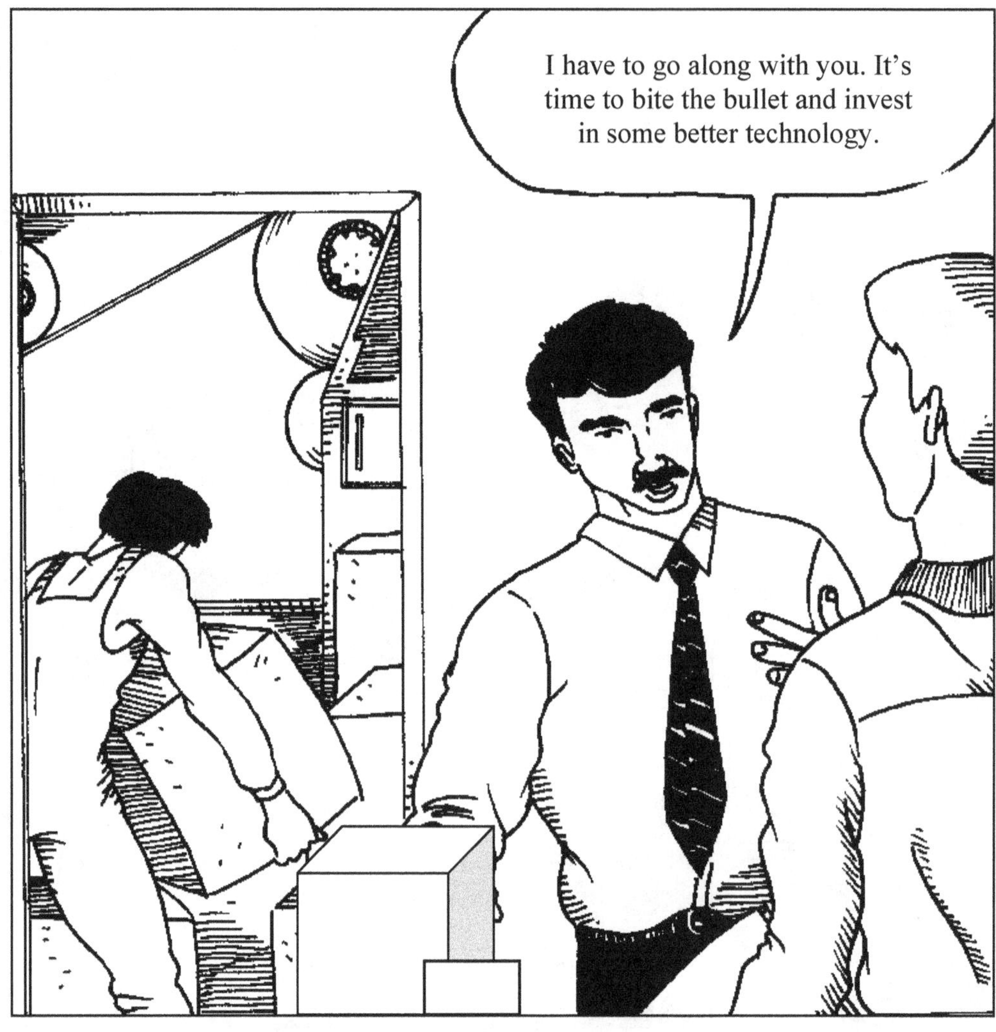

I have to go along with you. It's time to bite the bullet and invest in some better technology.

Unit 4 - TECHNOLOGY AND BUSINESS – Part 1

We live in a fast changing world. Think about some of the changes you have seen in your lifetime. In this unit you will listen to a conversation about changes in technology and business. Before you listen, match the following words with the correct meaning below.

changeover	slave	industry	costly

a person controlled by someone/something __________ change to a new system __________________

a branch of production/manufacture _______________ expensive/costing a lot of money ___________

Now listen to this conversation in which the manager of a company is talking to his assistant about making changes in the business. The conversation contains colloquial or everyday expressions which will be explained later in the unit - so don't worry if you don't understand every word. This time you are only listening for a general understanding of the topic. As you listen, tick the correct answers below. (There may be more than one correct answer.) When you have finished you can check your answers on page 115.

1) The Manager wants to talk to Kim, his assistant, because:

a) business is improving.

b) business is not going well.

2) The industry they are working in is:

a) the music industry.

b) the printing industry.

c) the toy making industry.

3) The manager has decided to:

a) invest in some better technology.

b) move the business to another factory.

c) apply for a better job.

4) The manager:

a) is happy about changing technology.

b) thinks we are becoming slaves to technology.

Now we'll look at the everyday expressions used in the conversation - turn to the next page.

CONVERSATION 1 (with everyday expressions)

Read this conversation as you listen to the audio cassette. Do you know what the *underlined* words mean? They are colloquial or 'everyday' expressions.

Manager: Oh Kim! Do you have a minute? I'd like to discuss a few things with you .... As you know, sales have been ***falling off*** over the past few months...and ***between you and me***, things aren't looking very good.

Assistant: Well.....

Manager: Look, before you say anything, I'm not ***pointing the finger*** at you. I know you've suggested several times that we need to ***go in for*** better equipment, if we're going to ***hold our own*** in the industry. And I have to ***go along with*** you now. It's time to ***bite the bullet*** and invest in some better technology.

Assistant: That's great news. I'm sure it's the right move.

Manager: Well, as you've pointed out, we're ***up against*** some strong competition in the printing industry and a lot of small businesses are ***folding.*** If we don't ***jump on the bandwagon*** now, we could very likely ***go under*** as well.

Assistant: I agree, absolutely. The thing is, you have to be ***at the cutting edge*** of change, if you want to stay in business these days.

Manager: That's for sure and you have to ***keep your finger on the pulse***. You know, I've been ***putting off*** making the changes because I know it'll be costly, not only in equipment, but in training too. But ***the bottom line*** is, if we don't spend money, we won't make any.

Assistant: That's very true. So when do you think we'll start the changeover?

Manager: ***The sooner the better***, I suppose. There're some big changes to make and I'm not really looking forward to them. You know .... I wonder whether all this new technology is really making our lives easier. It seems to me we've created ***a vicious circle***......

Assistant: What do you mean?

Manager: Well, technology's supposed to have given us more time and freedom but it seems we're becoming slaves to technology.....

Assistant: Mm. I hadn't thought of it that way.

Manager: But then maybe I just don't like change...It's ***mind-boggling*** the way technology is changing! No sooner do I ***get my head around*** something new, than it changes again!

Assistant: Well, I know what you mean but I think we have to ***go with the flow*******.** whether we like it or not ...

Manager: I suppose so ...Well, I'd better ***get the ball rolling***. I'll start making some phone calls now.

If we don't jump on the bandwagon now, we could go under as well.

Now let's see what these expressions mean - look at the next page.

CONVERSATION 2 (explanation of everyday expressions)

Compare Conversation 1 with Conversation 2 **-You will see that some of the words are different but the meaning is the same in both conversations. Find the underlined words in Conversation 1, then underline the words with the same meaning in Conversation 2. For example: *falling off* (Conversation 1) = *decreasing* (Conversation 2)**

Manager: Oh Kim! Do you have a minute? I'd like to discuss a few things with you .... As you know, sales have been decreasing over the past few months... and confidentially (this information is private), things aren't looking very good.

Assistant: Well.....

Manager: Look, before you say anything, I'm not saying the problem was caused by you. I know you've suggested several times that we need to get/seek better equipment if we're going to keep/defend our position in the industry. And I have to agree with you now. It's time to make an important/difficult decision and invest in some better technology.

Assistant: That's great news. I'm sure it's the right move.

Manager: Well, as you've pointed out, we're competing with some strong competition in the printing industry and a lot of small businesses are failing/closing. If we don't follow the popular course now, we could very likely fail as well.

Assistant: I agree, absolutely. The thing is, you have to be involved in the most advanced/recent developments of change, if you want to stay in business these days.

Manager: That's for sure and you have to know the latest information. You know, I've been delaying making the changes because I know it'll be costly, not only in equipment, but in training too. But the basic truth is, if we don't spend money, we won't make any.

Assistant: That's very true. So when do you think we'll start the changeover?

Manager: As soon as possible, I suppose. There're some big changes to make and I'm not really looking forward to them. You know .... I wonder whether all this new technology is really making our lives easier. It seems to me we've created a cycle in which the solution to one problem has created more problems.

Assistant: What do you mean?

Manager: Well, technology's supposed to have given us more time and freedom but it seems we're becoming slaves to technology.....

Assistant: Mm. I hadn't thought of it that way.

Manager: But then maybe I just don't like change...It's unbelievable/amazing the way technology is changing! No sooner do I understand/accept something new, than it changes again!

Assistant: Well, I know what you mean but I think we have to accept changes (in life)..... whether we like it or not ...

Manager: I suppose so...Well, I'd better start the project/activity. I'll start making some phone calls now.

Now to become familiar with the everyday expressions, practise reading CONVERSATION 1 aloud with a partner.

Unit 4 - TECHNOLOGY AND BUSINESS – Part 3

Listen to the conversation again and fill in the missing words. You may have to listen more than once. (Don't worry about your spelling as this exercise focuses on listening skills - you can check your spelling later.)

Manager: Oh Kim! Do you have a minute? I'd like to discuss a few things with you .... As you know, sales have been ________***off*** over the past few months...and ________***you and me***, things aren't looking very good.

Assistant: Well.....

Manager: Look, before you say anything, I'm not ***pointing the*** ________at you. I know you've suggested several times that we need to ***go in for*** better equipment if we're going to ***hold our*** ______in the industry. And I have to ______***along with*** you now. It's time to ________***the bullet*** and invest in some better technology.

Assistant: That's great news. I'm sure it's the right move.

Manager: Well, as you've pointed out, we're ____***against*** some strong competition in the printing industry and a lot of small businesses are ***folding***. If we don't ______***on the bandwagon*** now, we could very likely ***go*** ________as well.

Assistant: I agree, absolutely. The thing is, you have to be ***at the cutting edge*** of change, if you want to stay in business these days.

Manager: That's for sure and you have to ***keep your*** ________ ***on the pulse***. You know, I've been ***putting*** _____making the changes because I know it'll be costly, not only in equipment, but in training too. But ***the bottom*** _______is, if we don't spend money, we won't make any.

Assistant: That's very true. So when do you think we'll start the changeover?

Manager: ***The sooner the*** ________, I suppose. There're some big changes to make and I'm not really looking forward to them. You know .... I wonder whether all this new technology is really making our lives easier. It seems to me we've created ***a vicious*** ________......

Assistant: What do you mean?

Manager: Well, technology's supposed to have given us more time and freedom but it seems we're becoming slaves to technology.....

Assistant: Mm. I hadn't thought of it that way.

Manager: But then maybe I just don't like change...It's ________***-boggling*** the way technology is changing! No sooner do I ***get my head*** ________ something new, than it changes again!

Assistant: Well, I know what you mean but I think we have to _____***with the flow***....... whether we like it or not ...

Manager: I suppose so......Well, I'd better ***get the*** ______ ***rolling***. I'll start making some phone calls now.

Now check your answers by comparing this page with CONVERSATION 1

Unit 4 - TECHNOLOGY AND BUSINESS – Part 4

In order to become more familiar with these new everyday expressions:

1) **Listen to Conversation 1 again and tick the boxes ☐ next to the expressions as you hear them.**
2) **After the conversation has finished, write in the definitions you can remember. Some have been done for you as examples.**
3) **Check your answers by turning to page 129.**

☐ falling off..

☐ between you and me ....

☐ pointing the finger...

☐ go in for............................*get/seek/show interest in (something)*...............................

☐ *hold our own..........................*keep/defend our position*...

☐ go along with...

☐ bite the bullet...

☐ up against ....*competing with*...

☐ folding..

☐ jump on the bandwagon..

☐ go under..

☐ *(be) at the cutting edge............*be involved with the most advanced/recent developments*...

☐ *keep your finger on the pulse..

☐ *putting off...

☐ the bottom line...

☐ the sooner the better..

☐ a vicious circle..............*a cycle in which the solution to a problem creates more problems*

☐ *mind-boggling...

☐ get my head around...............*understand/accept*...

☐ go with the flow..

☐ get the ball rolling...

LANGUAGE NOTES:

* The expression '***hold our own***' can also be expressed using other pronouns.
eg. 'hold *your* own' (keep/defend *your* position), 'hold *her* own' (keep *her* position) etc.

* '***at the cutting edge***' can also be expressed as, '***on the cutting edge***'.

* '***keep*** our finger on the pulse', can also be expressed as '***have*** our finger on the pulse'.

* '***put off***' (postpone) can be used before a noun, (eg. Don't ***put off*** the appointment). We can also say, 'Don't ***put*** the appointment ***off***.' When used with a pronoun, the pronoun goes in the middle of the expression. eg. Don't ***put*** it ***off***.

* We say something is '***mind-boggling***' when we think it is amazing, strange or difficult to understand. We also say that something '***boggles the mind***'.

Unit 4 - TECHNOLOGY AND BUSINESS– Part 5

LANGUAGE REVIEW

Complete the sentences, choosing from the everyday expressions which are listed below. You can use the clues in brackets ( ) at the end of each sentence to help you. Then complete the crossword using the everyday expressions you have written. The first one has been done as an example.

hold your own	cutting edge	go in for	mind boggling	vicious circle	get the ball rolling
~~go under~~	point the finger	up against	put off	finger on the pulse	bottom line

ACROSS

1) Our business will ***go under***, if our sales don't improve soon. (fail/ close)

3) Don't worry. With your excellent service and cheaper prices, you will ____ ______ _______ when the new shopping centre opens. (keep your position)

5) I can't ______ ____ going to the dentist any longer, my tooth is aching badly. (delay)

7) He is an excellent lawyer because he has his _________ ___ _____ _______. (knows the most recent information)

9) The scientists who made the new discovery were at the _________ ______ of research. (involved in the most recent developments)

11) We'll have to ____ ____ _____ ___________ today, if we are going to finish the job by next week. (start the project)

DOWN

2) Some people _______ ____ _________ at the government for the increase in crime. (blame)

4) He was ___ _________some good players, but he won the competition. (competing with)

6) It is ______ ___________ to think that life may exist on other planets. (amazing)

8) The _______ ______ is that many companies fail because they don't plan for future changes. (basic truth)

10) The economy has created a ________ ________ . There are less jobs because people aren't spending money. People aren't spending money because the economy isn't creating jobs. (a cycle of problems)

12) We are leaders in our industry because we ___ ___ _____ the most recent equipment as soon as its available on the market. (get/seek/show interest in)

2 8 12

1 g o * u n d e r 3

5 6 10

4

7

9

11

Answers page 115.

Unit 4 - TECHNOLOGY AND BUSINESS – Part 6

FOCUS ON SPOKEN LANGUAGE – PRONUNCIATION

A) Hearing and Pronouncing Syllables correctly
What is a syllable?

Spoken words are formed with ***syllables*** (or sounds).
A syllable is one unit of unbroken sound, usually containing ***a vowel sound.***

For example, s*u*n, h*e*lp, cr*y*, h*ou*se all have ***a vowel sound***, therefore each word is ***one syllable***. (In the word 'h*ou*se', the letters '***ou***' form ***one sound,*** the letter '*e*' at the end is ***not*** sounded, so it is not a syllable. Therefore, the word '***house***' has only one syllable).

Words such as *open, water*, *repeat* have two syllables. eg. ***o/pen; wa/ter, re/peat.***
The word, *anywhere,* has three syllables, ***a/ny/where,*** (*y* is pronounced as a vowel sound).

It's important to be able to ***hear*** how many syllables a word contains in order to be able to pronounce it correctly.

LISTENING PRACTICE

- Listen to the first part of Conversation 1 (below) again. As you listen, decide how many syllables the underlined words contain.
- Write each of the underlined word in the correct column below. One has been done as an example. (Answers: p 115)

Manager: Oh Kim! Do you have a ***minute?*** I'd like to ***discuss*** a few things with you.... As you ***know***, ***sales*** have been ***falling*** off over the past few ***months***...and ***between*** you and me, things aren't looking very ***good***.
Assistant: Well.....
Manager: Look, ***before*** you say ***anything***, I'm not pointing the ***finger*** at you. I know you've ***suggested*** several times that we need to go in for better equipment if we're going to hold our own in the ***industry***. And I have to go ***along*** with you now. It's time to bite the bullet and invest in some ***better technology***.

words with one syllable	words with two syllables	words with three syllables	words with four syllables
	dis/cuss		

Unit 4 - TECHNOLOGY AND BUSINESS – Part 6

FOCUS ON SPOKEN LANGUAGE
PRONUNCIATION - ***Hearing and Using Syllable Stress (continued)***

In words with more than one syllable, one sound is usually stronger (spoken more clearly) than the other. Knowing and using the right stress in words is essential to correct pronunciation.

Word Stress refers to the strongest (primary) sound in words of more than one syllable.

Important Note
A good dictionary will provide very useful information on how to pronounce words correctly. At the beginning of your dictionary, near the Pronunciation Key, you will see an explanation of how ***word stress*** is shown on all words listed in the dictionary.

Dictionaries use various symbols to show which syllable should be stressed, so it's important to check which symbol ***your*** dictionary uses. For example, in the word *open* (which contains two syllables), the stress is on the first syllable. Look at the way this may be shown in a dictionary.

*some dictionaries show a small stress mark ***' before and above*** the stressed syllable. eg. 'open.
*some dictionaries show a small stress mark ***' after and above*** the stressed syllable. eg. o'pen.
*some dictionaries use ***a line under*** the stressed syllable, to show the stressed sound. eg. ***o*** pen

To avoid confusion, always check which symbol *your* dictionary uses.

How does ***your*** dictionary show that the first syllable is stressed in the word *open*? _________

DICTIONARY PRACTICE
B) Using your dictionary, check the following two syllable words and show the stressed syllable, using the symbol from your dictionary. (Answers, page 116).
Then check if you can hear the stress, by listening to the words in Conversation 1 again.

minute ***between*** ***before*** ***finger*** ***along***

Look at the following words from Conversation 1 of this unit. Decide how many syllables each word contains and mark the stressed syllable. Then check your dictionary to see if you have marked the stress correctly.

anything ***suggested*** ***industry*** ***technology***

QUESTIONS TO ASK WHEN BUYING A DICTIONARY

Does the dictionary give a clear and simple definition of a word or expression?
Does the dictionary have a pronunciation key which is easy to understand, giving clear examples of pronunciation?
Does the dictionary have a simple way of showing syllable stress?
Does it show the part of speech (eg. verb, noun, adjective etc.)?

A good dictionary can provide you with very useful information and help you to become an independent learner but it is not a substitute for listening and talking to native speakers.

FOCUS ON SPOKEN LANGUAGE
C) Discourse Markers

In spoken language, speakers use various expressions to show connection between what has been said before and what is going to be said next.
For example:

- Expressions such as *'however', 'but', 'on the other hand',* show that ***a contrasting idea*** is going to be introduced into the conversation.
- Expressions like, *'I suppose..', 'I think..',* indicate that the speaker is going to give ***an opinion***.
- Some expressions are used to ***focus attention*** on what will be said next. eg. *'Well, you know..'*

Look at the following section from Conversation 1. Notice the expressions that the speakers use to ***focus attention*** on what they are going to say next.

Assistant: I agree, absolutely. ***The thing is***, you have to be at the cutting edge of change, if you want to stay in business these days.
Manager: That's for sure and you have to keep your finger on the pulse. ***You know***, I've been putting off making the changes because I know it'll be costly, not only in equipment, but in training too. ***But the bottom line is***, if we don't spend money, we won't make any.

Expressions like these are sometimes called ***discourse markers.*** They are an important part of everyday conversation, as they give signals about the kind of information that will come next.

Various expressions also ***show the attitude of the speaker*** to what they are talking about.

- Listen to the following section from Conversation 1 and fill in the missing expressions.
- What do the expressions show about the Manager's ***attitude*** to changing technology?

Assistant: .... So when do you think we'll start the changeover?
Manager: The sooner the better, __________. There're some big changes to make and I'm not really looking forward to them. You know .... __________whether all this new technology is really making our lives easier. ______________that we've created a vicious circle......
Assistant: What do you mean?
Manager: Well, technology's supposed to have given us more time and freedom but _____________we're becoming slaves to technology.....

Answers, page 116.

Expressions like, *'I suppose...', 'I wonder..', 'it seems...',* as well as introducing a personal opinion, give the impression that the manager may be a little ***uncertain/apprehensive*** about changes in technology and business.

Unit 4 - TECHNOLOGY AND BUSINESS – Part 6

FOCUS ON SPOKEN LANGUAGE
Discourse Markers (continued)

As you look at the conversations in other units of this book, you will see further examples of the way speakers use expressions which indicate their attitude to the topic of conversation as well as to show connection between what has just been said and what will come next.

Some examples are:

'*Well…*' is sometimes used when *offering an alternative* (Unit 1)

'Besides...', is used to introduce an *additional reason* (Unit 2)

'*Actually…*' is used to introduce an *important remark or expectation* (Unit 3, Unit 8)

'And of course,….', is used to indicate an *additional important argument* (Unit 5)

'Not necessarily…' is used to indicate *doubt or disagreement* with a prediction (Unit 6)

'Fair enough…' is used to show *understanding/acceptance* of a choice or opinion. (Unit 7)

'As far as I'm concerned,….. ' introduces an opinion. (Unit 9)

'Really?....' is often used to get *confirmation* and often *precedes another question.* (Unit 10)

As mentioned earlier, these types of expressions are an important part of everyday conversation. They focus on what will come next and connect our ideas and opinions. Without them our conversation would not sound natural.

D) 'the......er, the better'

In Conversation 1, when the manager was asked when the changeover to new technology would start, he answered, ***'The sooner the better'***, meaning,' I'd prefer it to happen ***as soon as possible***'. The pattern, ***'the......er, the better'*** can also be used in other expressions. For example:

'the earli***er*** the better' = 'I'd prefer it as early as possible'

Using the above pattern, complete the following table:

'I'd prefer it as hot as possible.'	means 'the ***hotter*** the better'
'I'd prefer it as light as possible.'	means 'the ________ the better'
'I'd prefer it as small as possible.'	means 'the ________ the better'
'I'd prefer it as clear as possible.'	means 'the ________ the better'

Answers page 116.

NOTES

UNIT 5

TALKING ABOUT POLITICS AND GOVERNMENT

Unit 5 - TALKING ABOUT POLITICS AND GOVERNMENT - Part 1

Australia has a democratic form of government. In other words, the people choose the government they want to represent them through a free electoral system. Before you listen to the following conversation about politics and government, check the meaning of the words below in a dictionary.

democracy	term	party	issue	priority	criticise

Write the word next to its correct meaning below; then check your answers on page 116.

period of time in government _________ a political group_________________________
first choice, importance _____________ important subject_________________________
government by the people____________ judge, find faults _________________________

In this unit you will listen to a conversation between friends, Ali and Majid, who are talking about politics just before an election. The conversation contains colloquial or everyday expressions that will be explained later in the unit - so don't worry if you don't understand every word. This time you are only listening for a general understanding of the topic. As you listen, tick the correct answers below. (There may be more than one correct answer.)

Answers page 116.

1) Ali (the first speaker) is confused about:

a) who to vote for.

b) where to vote.

2) Ali thinks the government should give priority to:

a) health.

b) education.

c) employment.

3) Majid suggests that:

a) Ali should write an article for the newspaper

b) Ali should become a politician.

Now we'll look at the everyday expressions used in the conversation - turn to the next page.

CONVERSATION 1 (with everyday expressions)

Read this conversation as you listen to the audio tape. Do you know what the *underlined* words mean? They are colloquial or 'everyday' expressions.

Ali: You know, I still can't ***make up my mind*** who to vote for. They all ***promise the earth*** in the ***run-up to*** an election. It's quite confusing, trying to make the right decision.

Majid: That's for sure. And of course, the question is, will they ***live up to*** their promises once they're voted in? They ***pay lip service to*** the problems before the elections but often ***haven't got much to show*** when their term***'s up.***

Ali: Mm, you've got a point, but I'd prefer to focus on future issues now. For example, I want a government that'll give students ***a fair go*** so it's important for me to know which party'll make education a priority.

Majid: Yeah, but don't you think all politicians make promises at election time and worry about how they're going to ***deliver the goods*** later. I think ***it's six of one and half a dozen of the other*** who we vote for. One vote won't make a difference anyway.

Ali: I can't agree with you there, Majid. I think every vote's important in a democracy. Look, I know we all ***knock*** the ***pollies*** sometimes but I do think some of them ***give it their best shot***. And if they don't do a good job, they have to ***face the music*** at the next election. The thing is, we have to ***weigh up*** all the promises, ***see through*** the ***hype*** and make an informed decision about who we think'll do the best job, and as I said, that's not easy.

Majid: You're right there. I suppose I should stop ***whinging*** and ***sit up and take notice*** from now on. Hey, Ali you're pretty ***cluey***, why don't you go into politics?

Ali: ***No way!***

'The thing is, we have to ***weigh up*** all the promises, ***see through*** the ***hype*** and make an informed decision about who we think'll do the best job.'

Now let's see what these expressions mean - look at the next page.

CONVERSATION 2 (explanation of everyday expressions)

Compare Conversation 1 with Conversation 2 **-You will see that some of the words are different but the meaning is the same in both conversations. Find the underlined words in Conversation 1, then underline the words with the same meaning in Conversation 2. eg. make up my mind (Conversation 1) = decide (Conversation 2)**

Ali: You know, I still can't decide who to vote for. They all promise great things in the period of time before an election. It's quite confusing, trying to make the right decision.

Majid: That's for sure. And, of course, the question is, will they honour/fulfil their promises once they're voted in? They talk without really meaning what they say about the problems before the elections but often haven't produced any results when their term is finished.

Ali: Mm, you've got a point, but I'd prefer to focus on future issues now. For example, I want a government that'll give students fair treatment so it's important for me to know which party'll make education a priority.

Majid: Yes, but don't you think all politicians make promises at election time and worry about how they're going to produce the promised results later. I think there will be no difference in the final result so it doesn't matter who we vote for. One vote won't make a difference anyway.

Ali: I can't agree with you there, Majid. I think every vote's important in a democracy. Look, I know we all criticise the politicians sometimes but I do think some of them try to achieve the best result. And if they don't do a good job, they have to accept responsibility and criticism at the next election. The thing is, we have to consider carefully all the promises, not be deceived by all the publicity and make an informed decision about who we think'll do the best job, and as I said, that's not easy.

Majid: You're right there. I suppose I should stop complaining and become interested from now on. Hey, Ali you're pretty clever, why don't you go into politics?

Ali: I would never do that!

Now to become familiar with the everyday expressions, practise reading CONVERSATION 1 aloud with a partner.

Unit 5 - TALKING ABOUT POLITICS AND GOVERNMENT - Part 3

Listen to the conversation again and fill in the missing words. You may have to listen more than once. (Don't worry about your spelling as this exercise focuses on listening skills - you can check your spelling later.)

Ali: You know, I still can't ***make*** ______ ***my mind*** who to vote for. They all ***promise the*** ________ in the ***run-up to*** an election. It's quite confusing, trying to make the right decision.

Majid: That's for sure. And of course, the question is, will they ________ ***up to*** their promises once they're voted in? They ***pay*** ______ ***service to*** the problems before the elections but often ***haven't got much to show*** when their term'***s*** ______.

Ali: Mm, you've got a point, but I'd prefer to focus on future issues now. For example, I want a government that'll give students ***a fair*** ______ so it's important for me to know which party'll make education a priority.

Majid: Yeah, but don't you think all politicians make promises at election time and worry about how they're going to ***deliver the*** ________ later. I think ***it's*** ______ ***of one and half a dozen of the other*** who we vote for. One vote won't make a difference anyway.

Ali: I can't agree with you there, Majid. I think every vote's important in a democracy. Look, I know we all ________ the ***pollies*** sometimes but I do think some of them ***give it their best*** ______. And if they don't do a good job, they have to ***face the*** ________ at the next election. The thing is, we have to ***weigh up*** all the promises, ______ ***through*** the ***hype*** and make an informed decision about who we think'll do the best job, and as I said, that's not easy.

Majid: You're right there. I suppose I should stop ***whinging*** and __________ ***and take notice*** from now on. Hey, Ali you're pretty ***cluey***, why don't you go into politics?

Ali: ***No*** ______ ***!***

Now check your answers by comparing this page with CONVERSATION 1

Unit 5 - TALKING ABOUT POLITICS AND GOVERNMENT - Part 4

In order to become more familiar with these new everyday expressions:

1) **Listen to Conversation 1 again and tick the boxes ☐ next to the expressions as you hear them.**
2) **After the conversation has finished, write in the definitions you can remember. Some have been done for you as an examples.**
3) **Check your answers by turning to page 130.**

☐ make up my mind ....

☐ promise the earth ....

☐ (the) run-up to.......... *period of time before (an event)*..........

☐ live up to (a promise).......... *honour/fulfil (a promise)*..........

☐ pay lip service to..........

☐ haven't got much to show ....

☐ (term) is up .... *term or time is finished / completed*..........

☐ a fair go ....

☐ deliver the goods .... *produce the promised results*..........

☐ six of one and half a dozen of the other ..... *there will be no difference in the final result*......

☐ knock ....

☐ pollies..........

☐ give it their best shot..........

☐ face the music..........

☐ weigh up..........

☐ see through .... *not be deceived by (someone or something)*.....

☐ hype ....

☐ whinging ....

☐ sit up and take notice.......... *become interested*..........

☐ cluey..........

☐ No way!..........

LANGUAGE NOTES:

*The expression ***'see through' (something or someone)*** is used in this Unit to mean ***'not be deceived by (something)'***. However, the expression ***'see (something) through,'*** used in Unit 2 - 'Talking about Study Problems' means ***'continue with a project until completion'***.

*Australians have a tendency to shorten words and add ***'ie'*** to the end of words. For example, you will hear ***Aussie*** meaning ***Australian***, and ***pollies*** meaning ***politicians***. For more examples, see page 125 of this book.

LANGUAGE REVIEW

Complete the sentences, choosing from the everyday expressions which are listed below.
You can use the clues in brackets ( ) at the end of each sentence to help you.
Then complete the crossword using the everyday expressions you have written.
The first one has been done as an example.

~~make up my mind~~	promise the earth	best shot	pays lip service	whinging
knock live up to	cluey	saw through	deliver the goods	fair go hype

ACROSS

1) I can't ***make up my mind*** which colour to paint my kitchen walls. (decide)
3) The taxpayers say they are not getting a _________ _____from the government. (fair treatment)
5) I don't know if I can do it, but I'll give it my _______ _______. (try to achieve the best result)
7) That company _______ ______ __________ to environmental issues but they are really only interested in making money. (talks without meaning what they say)
9) John will know the answer. He's very ________. (clever)
11) The council has promised a big new car park before Christmas but nobody believes they can __________ ______ ________. (produce the promised results)
13) Don't ________ another person's idea until you have thought about it carefully. (criticise)

DOWN

2) I'm sorry. I can't _______ _____ ____ my promise to have the job finished by tomorrow. (fulfil)
4) Politicians often __________ ______ ________ before an election. (promise great things)
6) The government has promised to improve public transport but I think it's just _________ before the election. (publicity)
8) The salesman said the car was working perfectly but I ______ __________ his lies. (was not deceived by)
10) You're always ___________ about having no money! Why don't you get a job? (complaining)

1 m a k e * u p * m y * m i n d

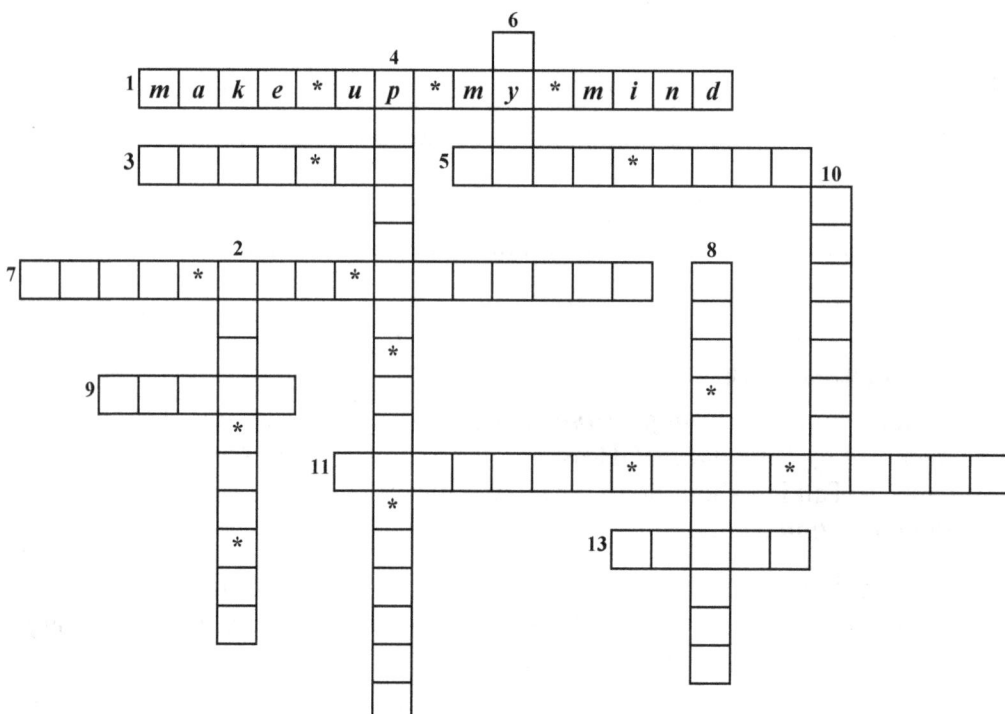

Answers page 116.

Unit 5 - TALKING ABOUT POLITICS AND GOVERNMENT - Part 6

FOCUS ON SPOKEN LANGUAGE- CONVERSATION STRATEGIES

A) Agreeing and disagreeing politely

In Conversation1, Ali and Majid agreed about some things but didn't agree on every point during their discussion.

Read Conversation 1 and find the expressions which the speakers used to introduce points of agreement and disagreement. Write them in the appropriate column below.
Two have been done as examples. Answers, page 117.

Expressions showing agreement	*Expressions showing disagreement*
That's for sure.	***you've got a point but......***

When ***disagreeing*** with another person's opinion, expressions such as, '*You've got a point but....*' and '*Yes, but don't you think......*' demonstrate politeness by ***showing that you have listened*** to the other person's opinion before giving a different opinion.

Note: In Conversation 1, the expression, *'No way!'* is used in a friendly, joking way. However, when used with a strong tone, this expression can indicate strong disagreement, so be careful how and when you use it.

Other ways of ***disagreeing politely*** are:

Yes, but I think..............

Yes, but on the other hand......

I agree to an extent but.......... (means: I don't agree completely)

Unit 5 - TALKING ABOUT POLITICS AND GOVERNMENT - Part 6

FOCUS ON SPOKEN LANGUAGE
B) Using Pronouns

Pronouns (words such as *I, you, they, she, him, we, it, etc.*) are often used in English as a ***substitute*** for ***previously mentioned names or things (nouns)***. To repeat the name continually sounds very unnatural.

For example, we say: 'Where is ***Sam***(noun)? I told ***him***(pronoun) to come as soon as possible. ***He***(pronoun)'s in trouble.'

We ***do not*** say: 'Where is ***Sam***(noun)? I told ***Sam***(noun) to come as soon as possible. ***Sam***(noun)'s in trouble.

The pronoun 'They'

In spoken English, pronouns also sometimes refer to a person or thing (noun) which has ***not*** been previously mentioned but is 'understood' between the speakers. For example, in Conversation 1 the speakers both use ***'they'*** at the beginning of their conversation to refer to 'politicians'. They understood that *'they'* referred to *'politicians'* because the topic was about the election.

PRACTICE

Look at the following sentences. Who does ***they*** refer to in each sentence? Answers: page 117.

1) I applied for the job two weeks ago. I wonder when ***they***'ll contact me.

   They refers to ___________________________________

2) ***They*** used to think the earth was the centre of the universe.

   They refers to ___________________________________

3) ***They***'re always moving things around in this supermarket.

   They refers to ___________________________________

'It'

The pronoun '***it***' can also be used at the beginning of a sentence to refer to something which is understood by the speakers to mean '***the situation we are talking about***' or '***this situation***'.

For example, you will read in line 2 of Conversation 1 that Ali says:

It's quite confusing, trying to make the right decision.

This means: ***This situation*** (trying to make the right decision about who to vote for) is quite confusing.

Look at some more examples:

It's amazing!	= The situation we are talking about is amazing.
It's clear he doesn't want to do the job.	= The situation is clear. He doesn't want the job.
It's beautiful here, isn't it?	= This situation is beautiful, isn't it?'

Unit 5 - TALKING ABOUT POLITICS AND GOVERNMENT - Part 6

FOCUS ON SPOKEN LANGUAGE
C) Pronouns - pronunciation and spelling

In spoken language, pronouns are often followed by a contraction.
For example, *'he is'* becomes *he's*; *'we are'* becomes *we're*; *'they are'* becomes *they're.*
These particular pronouns are often confused with other words which have the same pronunciation. Look at the ***underlined*** words in the following sentence from Conversation 1.

And of course, the question is, will they live up to ***their*** promises once ***they're*** voted in?

If you listen to this sentence, you will see that ***their*** and ***they're*** are pronounced similarly. However, they have different meanings: ***their*** shows possession; ***they're*** = they are.

Look at the following sentences. The ***bold*** words in each sentence are pronounced the same.

- The dog has eaten ***its*** dinner and now ***it's*** sitting quietly in the corner.
  (***its*** shows possession; ***it's*** = it is)
- ***His*** mother said ***he's*** very lazy. (***his*** shows possession; ***he's*** = he is)
  Note: ***his*** is pronounced with a short vowel /hɪz/; ***he's*** is pronounced with a long vowel sound/hi:z/, however the correct usage of these words is often confused.
- ***You're*** clever because you always finish ***your*** homework first.
  (***you're*** = you are; ***your*** shows possession)
- We ***were*** too late yesterday to see the movie, so ***we're*** going to see the movie today.
  (***were*** is a past plural verb; ***we're*** = we are)

PRACTICE

Complete the following sentences, by choosing the correct word from the box and writing it in the appropriate space. Answers, page 117.

it's	*its*	*their*	*they're*	*were*	*we're*	*he's*	*his*	*you're*	*your*

1) ________very upset because we lost our camera when we _______ overseas last month.

2) ________very happy that he's passed ________ driving test!

3) _________ much taller than ________ sister but she's older than you, isn't she?

4) The cat has eaten ____ dinner and now _____sitting on the window sill.

5) _________ coming by train because _________car is being repaired.

UNIT 6

A NEW VENTURE - MAKING DECISIONS

Unit 6 - A NEW VENTURE – MAKING DECISIONS - Part 1

What's the biggest decision you have ever made? Did you have to think about it for a long time before you made your decision? In this unit you will hear expressions related to decision making. Before you listen, match the following words with the meaning below.

decisive	advantages	disadvantages	possibilities

benefits, good points ____________________ making definite decisions _______________

negative points ________________________ things that are possible ________________

Before making big decisions, people usually think about the *pros and cons* involved.
In other words, they consider the advantages and disadvantages of the venture.
Listen to this conversation between friends who are talking about a new venture. The conversation contains colloquial or everyday expressions which will be explained later in the unit - so don't worry if you don't understand every word. This time you are only listening for a general understanding of the topic. As you listen, tick the correct answers below. (There may be more than one correct answer.)
When you have finished you can check your answers on page 117.

1) What kind of business would Don like to start?
   a) a video shop.
   b) a coffee shop.
   c) a camera shop.

2) Where is the business he is interested in buying?
   a) Highland Street.
   b) High Street.
   c) Brighten Street.

3) Don plans to promote the business by having:
   a) special introductory prices.
   b) an 'Under New Management' sign.
   c) a party.

4) Kara suggests that before making a decision Don should:
   a) go to the bank.
   b) draw a plan.
   c) write a list of the pros and cons.

Now we'll look at the everyday expressions used in the conversation - turn to the next page.

Unit 6 - A NEW VENTURE – MAKING DECISIONS - Part 2A

CONVERSATION 1 (with everyday expressions)

Read this conversation as you listen to the audio tape. Do you know what the *underlined* words mean? They are colloquial or 'everyday' expressions.

Don: You know how I've been ***toying with the idea*** of starting my own coffee shop.

Kara: Yes, you've been talking about it for as long as I can remember.

Don: Well, the other day I was looking through the newspaper and I ***came across*** one for sale. It's the one on High Street; you know, near the corner. It's ***going for a song***. I'm seriously thinking about ***taking the plunge*** and buying it.

Kara: But I thought you wanted to start a business ***from scratch***.

Don: Well, I did. But buying one that's already ***up and running*** would make it easier. It'd save me a lot of time, money and hard work.

Kara: Mm, not necessarily. I heard ***on the grapevine*** that the business was ***going downhill*** and that's why they're trying to ***get rid of*** it.

Don: Yes, I know it's a bit ***run-down*** but a bit of ***elbow grease*** will fix that and I have a few ideas ***up my sleeve*** to get the new business ***off the ground***. I'll put up a big sign saying, 'Under New Management', and I'll have special introductory prices to bring in the customers. I think it'll go well.

Kara: Maybe, maybe not. Look, I'm not trying to ***put you off***. I just wouldn't want to see you ***get your fingers burnt***. If I were you, I'd write a list of the ***pros and cons*** of starting a business ***from scratch*** or buying one that's already established and ***weigh up*** the possibilities on both sides before making any decisions.

Don: Yes, that's a very good idea. Don't worry. I know there's a lot to ***take into account***. I'll ***look into it*** a lot more before I make a final decision. I know there are ***drawbacks*** on both sides but I'll ***do my homework*** before I ***go ahead*** with anything.

Kara: And let me know if there's anything I can do to help, won't you.

Don: Yes. I will, thanks.

Now let's see what these expressions mean - look at the next page.

Unit 6 - A NEW VENTURE – MAKING DECISIONS - Part 2B

CONVERSATION 2 (explanation of everyday expressions)

Compare Conversation 1 with Conversation 2 **-You will see that some of the words are different but the meaning is the same in both conversations. Find the underlined words in Conversation 1, then underline the words with the same meaning in Conversation 2. For example: *toying with the idea* (Conversation 1) = *thinking about* (Conversation 2)**

Don: You know how I've been thinking about starting my own coffee shop.

Kara: Yes, you've been talking about it for as long as I can remember.

Don: Well, the other day I was looking through the newspaper and I found by chance one for sale. It's the one on High Street; you know, near the corner. It's being sold very cheaply. I'm seriously thinking about taking the decisive step and buying it.

Kara: But I thought you wanted to start a business from the beginning (without help).

Don: Well, I did. But buying one that's already operating would make it easier. It'd save me a lot of time, money and hard work.

Kara: Mm, not necessarily. I heard through information from other people that the business was deteriorating/not doing well and that's why they're trying to dispose of it.

Don: Yes, I know it's a bit neglected/in a bad condition but a bit of hard work will fix that and I have a few ideas in my mind to get the new business into successful operation. I'll put up a big sign saying, 'Under New Management', and I'll have special introductory prices to bring in the customers. I think it'll go well.

Kara: Maybe, maybe not. Look, I'm not trying to discourage you/tell you not to do it. I just wouldn't want to see you suffer a bad experience (or lose money). If I were you, I'd write a list of the advantages and disadvantages of starting a business from the beginning or buying one that's already established and consider the possibilities on both sides before making any decisions.

Don: Yes, that's a very good idea. Don't worry. I know there's a lot to consider. I'll investigate a lot more before I make a final decision. I know there are disadvantages on both sides but I'll research thoroughly before I continue with anything.

Kara: And let me know if there's anything I can do to help, won't you.

Don: Yes. I will, thanks.

Now to become familiar with the everyday expressions, practise reading CONVERSATION 1 aloud with a partner.

Unit 6 - A NEW VENTURE – MAKING DECISIONS - Part 3

Listen to the conversation again and fill in the missing words. You may have to listen more than once. (Don't worry about your spelling as this exercise focuses on listening skills - you can check your spelling later.)

Don: You know how I've been ***toying with the*** ________ of starting my own coffee shop.

Kara: Yes, you've been talking about it for as long as I can remember.

Don: Well, the other day I was looking through the newspaper and I ________ ***across*** one for sale. It's the one on High Street; you know, near the corner. It's ***going for a song***. I'm seriously thinking about ***taking the*** ________ and buying it.

Kara: But I thought you wanted to start a business ***from*** ________.

Don: Well, I did. But buying one that's already ***up*** ________ would make it easier. It'd save me a lot of time, money and hard work.

Kara: Mm, not necessarily. I heard ***on the*** ________ that the business was ***going*** ________ and that's why they're trying to ***get rid of*** it.

Don: Yes, I know it's a bit ***run-down*** but a bit of ________ ***grease*** will fix that and I have a few ideas ***up my*** ________ to get the new business ***off the*** ________. I'll put up a big sign saying, 'Under New Management', and I'll have special introductory prices to bring in the customers. I think it'll go well.

Kara: Maybe, maybe not. Look, I'm not trying to ***put you*** ________. I just wouldn't want to see you ***get your*** ________ ***burnt***. If I were you, I'd write a list of the ***pros and cons*** of starting a business from scratch or buying one that's already established and ***weigh up*** the possibilities on both sides before making any decisions.

Don: Yes, that's a very good idea. Don't worry. I know there's a lot to ________ ***into account.*** I'll ***look*** ________ ***it*** a lot more before I make a final decision. I know there are ***drawbacks*** on both sides but I'll ***do my homework*** before I ***go ahead*** with anything.

Kara: And let me know if there's anything I can do to help, won't you.

Don: Yes. I will, thanks.

Now check your answers by comparing this page with CONVERSATION 1

Unit 6 - A NEW VENTURE – MAKING DECISIONS - Part 4

In order to become more familiar with these new everyday expressions:

1) **Listen to Conversation 1 again and tick the boxes ☐ next to the expressions as you hear them.**
2) **After the conversation has finished, write in the definitions you can remember. Some have been done as examples.**
3) **Check your answers by turning to page 131.**

☐ toying with the idea……………………………………………………………………………

☐ came across………………………*found by chance*………………………………………

☐ going for a song…………………………………………………………………………..

☐ taking the plunge…………………*taking the decisive step*………………………………

☐ from scratch……………………………………………………………………………

☐ up and running…………………………………………………………………………

☐ *on the grapevine………………… *(heard) through information from other people*…………

☐ going downhill…………………………………………………………………………

☐ get rid of…………………………*dispose of*…………………………………………..

☐ run-down………………………………………………………………………………

☐ elbow grease……………………………………………………………………………

☐ up my sleeve……………………………………………………………………………

☐ off the ground…………………………………………………………………………..

☐ *put (you) off……………………*discourage (you)*…………………………………………

☐ *get your fingers burnt…………………………………………………………………

☐ pros and cons…………………………………………………………………………...

☐ weigh up ………………………………………………………………………………

☐ take into account……………………………………………………………………….

☐ look into it………………………………………………………………………………

☐ drawbacks………………………………………………………………………………

☐ do (my) homework……………… *research/investigate*…………………………………

☐ go ahead………………………………………………………………………………...

LANGUAGE NOTE:

To hear something '***on the grapevine***' usually means that the information has come through several people before it has been told to you.

Note the different meaning between, ***to put someone off***, used in this Unit to mean ***discourage***, and the expression used in Unit 4, ***to put something off***, meaning to ***delay a decision/activity***.

The expression '***get your fingers burnt***' often refers to bad experiences involving money.

Note: ***burnt*** can be also be spelt ***burned*** and pronounced as /bɜːnt/ or /bɜːnd/.

Unit 6 - A NEW VENTURE – MAKING DECISIONS - Part 5

LANGUAGE REVIEW

Complete the sentences, choosing from the everyday expressions which are listed below.
You can use the clues in brackets ( ) at the end of each sentence to help you.
Then complete the crossword using the everyday expressions you have written.
The first one has been done as an example.

up and running	**~~come across~~**	**elbow grease**	**look into**	**put him off**	**toying with the idea**
going for a song	**off the ground**	**on the grapevine**	**get your fingers burnt**	**weigh up**	

ACROSS

1) Let me know if you ***come across*** a set of keys. I've lost my car keys. (find by chance)
3) We'll need plenty of _______ _________ to clean this oven. It's very dirty. (hard work)
5) Be careful when investing your money. You don't want to______ ________ ________ ___________. (suffer a bad experience)
7) Our new business will be ____ _____ _________ in a few weeks. (operating).
9) I'm _________ ______ ______ _______ of buying a new car soon. (considering)
11) I heard ____ ______ __________ that David and Sue are getting married. Is it true? (through information heard from other people)

DOWN

2) I bought this car because it was ________ ______ __ ______. I hope it goes well. (very cheap)
4) It's important to ______ ______ any new venture carefully before proceeding. (investigate)
6) You'll _____ ______ ____if you continue to say negative things. (discourage him)
8) There's lots of work to do before our new business gets ____ _____ _______(into successful operation)
10) It's important to ________ ____ the pros and cons before making big decisions. (consider)

1 c o m e * a c r o s s

2 3 4 5 6 7 8 9 10 11

Answers, page 118.

Unit 6 - A NEW VENTURE – MAKING DECISIONS - Part 6

FOCUS ON SPOKEN LANGUAGE

A) Using substitute words (pronouns) in place of nouns

As discussed in Unit 5, we substitute nouns (names of people and things) with pronouns (words such as, *'they', 'we', 'she')*. In this unit, the use of ***it*** and ***one*** as noun substitutes is analysed.

Look at the following section from Conversation 1.

Don:	You know how I've been toying with the idea of starting my own coffee shop.
Kara:	Yes, you've been talking about ***it*** for as long as I can remember.
Don:	Well, the other day I was looking through the newspaper and I came across ***one*** for sale. *It*'s the ***one*** on High Street; you know, near the corner. ***It***'s going for a song. I'm seriously thinking about taking the plunge and buying ***it***.

What do the ***underlined*** words **'*it*'** and **'*one*'** refer to?
The first sentence has been done as an example.

1) 'Yes, you've been talking about ***it*** for as long as I can remember'.

'*It*' refers to ***the idea of buying a coffee shop***.

2) I came across ***one*** for sale.

'*one*' refers to ____

3) **'*It*'**s the ***one*** on High Street; you know, near the corner'.

'*It*' refers to ______________________ **'*one*'** refers to ________________________________

4) **'*It*'**s going for a song. I'm seriously thinking about taking the plunge and buying ***it***'.

'*It*' refers to ______________________

Answers, page 118.

'***One***' can also be used in the plural form, '***ones***'. Look at these examples.

'I usually buy green ***apples***, but the red ***ones*** were better value this week'.
'I lost my new ***glasses***, so I'm lucky that I still had my old ***ones***'.

PRACTICE
Complete the following sentences, using '***one***' or '***ones***'. Answers, page 118.

'I want to buy a new dress for the party but I'm having trouble finding the right _______. I've seen some lovely _______ but I'd like to get ________ with long sleeves'.

Unit 6 - A NEW VENTURE – MAKING DECISIONS - Part 6

B) Giving Advice

When giving advice, we often use the pattern, '***If I were you, I would** + **verb......***'
For example, '***If I were you, I'd go*** to the doctor for a check up'.

Note that the contracted form ***'d*** is used in spoken language (rather than ***would***).

In Conversation 1, Kara gives Don some advice using this pattern.
Find and complete the following sentence from Conversation 1 (page 60).

> 'If I were you, ____
> ________________or buying one that's already established and weigh up the possibilities on both sides before making any decisions.'
>
> Answer, page 118.

We use this pattern when we want to be polite (not too dogmatic), when making suggestions.
This kind of sentence has two parts:

The part with ***if*** + ***past tense verb***......and the part with ***would*** + ***present simple verb.*** For example:

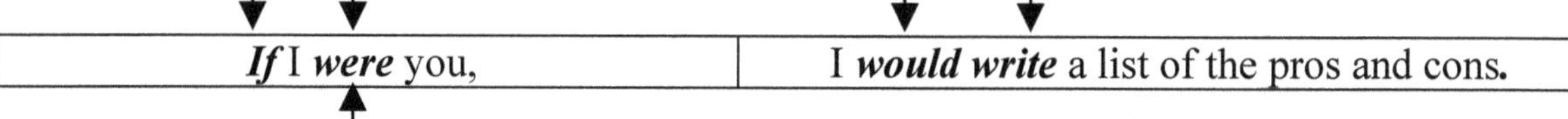

If I ***were*** you,	I ***would write*** a list of the pros and cons.

Notice that a ***past tense verb*** is used, though this sentence is referring to the ***future***.
Using a ***past tense verb*** with '***if***' makes the sentence less dogmatic/more polite.

Note: *'If I **was** you,...'* is also used when giving advice, however, *'If I **were** you,'* is more usual.

We also use this pattern in the ***negative*** form (would***n't***).

> ***eg. If*** I ***were*** you, I ***wouldn't go*** there without a lot of money.

C) Weighing up the pros and cons - talking about future possibilities

When we are trying to make a decision, we often talk about the ***possible*** results of a particular action. In other words, we say what is likely to happen, ***if*** we do a particular thing.
In these situations we use ***would*** + ***present simple verb***.

eg. 'I think it ***would be*** better to buy a new car rather than a second hand one. It ***would save*** money on repairs'.

Look at the following sentence from Conversation 1, in which Don talks about the possible advantages of buying the coffee shop on High Street.

> Don: ......'But buying one that's already up and running ***would make*** it easier.'

Don uses ***would*** + ***present simple verb*** in another sentence to talk about future possibilities.
Complete the following sentence from Conversation 1 (page 60).

> 'It ____ and hard work.'

Answer, page 118.

Unit 6 - A NEW VENTURE – MAKING DECISIONS - Part 6

FOCUS ON SPOKEN LANGUAGE

D) REVISION - Hearing and Pronouncing Syllables correctly

As discussed in Unit 4, it's important to be able to ***hear*** how many syllables a word contains in order to be able to pronounce it correctly. (You may need to check Part 6A & 6B of Unit 4 again, before doing the following revision exercise).

Revision Exercise

- Decide how many syllables the [boxed] words (below) contain, by using your dictionary or listening to this section of Conversation 1 on your audio-cassette as you read it.

Don:	You [know] how I've been [toying] with the [idea] of starting my own [coffee] shop.
Kara:	Yes, you've been talking [about] it for as long as I can [remember].
Don:	Well, the other day I was looking [through] the [newspaper] and I came across one for [sale]. It's the one on High Street; you know, near the corner. It's going for a song. I'm [seriously] thinking about taking the [plunge] and buying it.
Kara:	But I thought you wanted to start a [business] from scratch.

- Write each word in the correct column below.
  One has been done as an example. Answers, page 118.

words with one syllable	words with two syllables	words with three syllables	words with four syllables
know			

Syllable Stress

Now decide which syllable is ***stressed*** in each of the following words.

idea - the ***second (middle)*** syllable is stressed.

about - the _______________ syllable is stressed.

remember - the _______________ syllable is stressed.

seriously - the _______________ syllable is stressed

business - the _______________ syllable is stressed

Answers, page 119.

LANGUAGE REVIEW TWO

(Units 4 - 6)

This section reviews some of the expressions which were introduced in Units 4, 5, and 6 and gives you a chance to see what you have remembered.

Look at the pictures on the opposite page and decide what the people are saying by choosing from the expressions below.

Match each picture with an appropriate expression by writing the correct letter in the box next to each expression.

For extra practice, you could write the appropriate expression in the space provided in the picture.

1) Between you and me, I can't get my head around this modern art. ☐

2) I'm going to bite the bullet and apply for a business loan. ☐

3) The universe is so vast. It's mind-boggling! ☐

4) I don't know if I can do it but I'll give it my best shot. ☐

5) Look at this! It's going for a song! ☐

6) I know it's run down but a bit of elbow grease will fix it. ☐

7) I heard on the grapevine that they are getting engaged soon. ☐

8) The bottom line is, you must practise. Don't put it off any longer. ☐

9) I'm trying to weigh up which one is the best value. ☐

(Answers: page 119)

A
B
C
HOLIDAY GUIDES
ENGLISH
EXAM
6th NOV
D
E
F
CAR SALE
APPLICATION
G
H
I
THIS SIDE UP
DO IT YOURSELF
SHELVING
MANUAL

UNIT 7

TALKING ABOUT THE PAST

Unit 7 - TALKING ABOUT THE PAST - Part 1

In this unit you will hear someone talking about good memories, as well as a difficult situation in the past. In English there is an expression, 'Every cloud has a silver lining'. This means that every bad situation has some positive aspect. Do you agree with this expression?

Before you listen to the conversation, match the words in the box with the correct meanings below. Answers, page 119.

a shock	experiences	mischief	bitter	recover	independent

playful but unacceptable conduct __________	unhappy/angry because of problems ____________
a sudden, bad experience _________________	improve/return to a good situation _____________
being able to support yourself______________	things that happen to us during life _____________

Listen to the following conversation in which friends, who are working together, are talking about the past. (Unit 7 on your audio cassette.) The conversation contains colloquial or everyday expressions which will be explained later in the unit - so don't worry if you don't understand every word. This time you are only listening for a general understanding of the topic. As you listen, tick the correct answers below. (There may be more than one correct answer.) When you have finished you can check your answers on page 119.

1) When Dan (first speaker) was younger, he used to:

   a) party all weekend.

   b) work seven days a week.

   c) sleep most of the weekend.

2) One day he received the terrible news that:

   a) his parents had been killed in an accident.

   b) his friends had been killed in an accident.

   c) his grandmother had died.

3) Dan told his friend that:

   a) he had learnt a lot from his experiences.

   b) he would never recover from his experience.

Now we'll look at the everyday expressions used in the conversation - turn to the next page.

CONVERSATION 1 (with everyday expressions)

Read this conversation as you listen to the audio tape. Do you know what the *underlined* words mean? They are colloquial or 'everyday' expressions.

Dan: You know, whenever I hear that song, it ***takes me back to*** my younger days……..
We used to ***get up to*** some mischief. I'm surprised I'm still ***in one piece***!

Eve: What did you use to do?

Dan: We had a lot of fun but we did some ***crazy*** things! We used to ***burn the candle at both ends*** most weekends. We'd party all night and go straight to work the next day without any sleep.....or we'd ***take a sickie*** and go to the beach.

Eve: Really? How long did you ***keep that up***?

Dan: Oh, quite a while. I'd probably have kept it up a lot longer if my life hadn't been ***turned upside down*** one day by some terrible news.

Eve: Why? What happened to change things?

Dan: Well, I was at work one day when I received the news that my parents had been killed in a car accident.

Eve: Oh no, that's terrible. I'm so sorry. You haven't talked about that before. It must have been a terrible shock.

Dan: Yes, it was. It took me long time to ***get over it*** and I was very bitter for a while.... But I'd rather not ***go into it*** now.

Eve: ***Fair enough***...Well, you don't ***strike me as*** a bitter person now.

Dan: No, because one day someone said to me, 'We can let our experiences in life make us bitter or better' and I thought to myself, 'It's time to ***put this behind me*** and ***get on with*** the rest of my life'. And you know I ***haven't looked back*** since then.

Eve: Yes, we have to ***take the rough with the smooth***, don't we? We ***can't turn the clock back*** .

Dan: That's for sure. We all have our ***ups and downs*** in life. But you know, I've learnt a lot from that difficult time in my life. I learnt to ***stand on my own feet*** and that we never know what's ***around the corner***, so we should try to ***make the most of*** every day.

Eve: Yes, that's very true.

Now let's see what these expressions mean - look at the next page.

CONVERSATION 2 (explanation of everyday expressions)

Compare Conversation 1 with Conversation 2 **- You will see that some of the words are different but the meaning is the same in both conversations. Find the underlined words in Conversation 1, then underline the words with the same meaning in Conversation 2. For example: *takes me back* (Conversation 1) = *makes me remember* (Conversation 2)**

Dan: You know, whenever I hear that song, it makes me remember my younger days……... We used to do/be engaged in some mischief. I'm surprised I'm still alive and unharmed!

Eve: What did you use to do?

Dan: We had a lot of fun but we did some foolish (but exciting) things! We used to have very little sleep (because of too much activity) most weekends. We'd party all night and go straight to work the next day without any sleep.....or we'd take a day off work (with the excuse of being sick) and go to the beach.

Eve: Really? How long did you continue (that activity)?

Dan: Oh, quite a while. I'd probably have kept it up a lot longer if my life hadn't been completely changed one day by some terrible news.

Eve: Why? What happened to change things?

Dan: Well, I was at work one day when I received the news that my parents had been killed in a car accident.

Eve: Oh no, that's terrible. I'm so sorry. You haven't talked about that before. It must have been a terrible shock.

Dan: Yes, it was. It took me long time to recover and I was very bitter for a while...But I'd rather not talk about/discuss it now.

Eve: I understand...Well, you don't seem/appear to me as a bitter person now.

Dan: No, because one day someone said to me, 'We can let our experiences in life make us bitter or better' and I thought to myself, 'It's time to recover from this unhappy experience and proceed with the rest of my life'. And you know I have progressed/succeeded since then.

Eve: Yes, we have to accept both bad and good experiences in life, don't we? We can't go back to the past.

Dan: That's for sure. We all have good and bad experiences in life. But you know, I've learnt a lot from that difficult time in my life. I learnt to be independent and that we never know what's in the future, so we should try to fully use and enjoy every day.

Eve: Yes, that's very true.

Now to become familiar with the everyday expressions, practise reading CONVERSATION 1 aloud with a partner.

Unit 7 - TALKING ABOUT THE PAST - Part 3

Listen to the conversation again and fill in the missing words. You may have to listen more than once. (Don't worry about your spelling as this exercise focuses on listening skills - you can check your spelling later.)

Dan: You know, whenever I hear that song, it ***takes me ________ to*** my younger days……..
We used to ***get up to*** some mischief. I'm surprised I'm still ***in ________ piece***!

Eve: What did you use to do?

Dan: We had a lot of fun but we did some ***crazy*** things! We used to ***burn the ________ at both ends*** most weekends. We'd party all night and go straight to work the next day without any sleep.....or we'd ***take a ________*** and go to the beach.

Eve: Really? How long did you ***keep that ____***?

Dan: Oh, quite a while. I'd probably have kept it up a lot longer if my life hadn't been ***turned ________ down*** one day by some terrible news.

Eve: Why? What happened to change things?

Dan: Well, I was at work one day when I received the news that my parents had been killed in a car accident.

Eve: Oh no, that's terrible. I'm so sorry. You haven't talked about that before. It must have been a terrible shock.

Dan: Yes, it was. It took me long time to ***get ________ it*** and I was very bitter for a while....But I'd rather not ***go ________ it*** now.

Eve: ***Fair enough*** ...Well, you don't ________ ***me as*** a bitter person now.

Dan: No, because one day someone said to me, 'We can let our experiences in life make us bitter or better' and I thought to myself, 'It's time to ***put this ________ me*** and ***get on with*** the rest of my life'. And you know I ***haven't looked ________*** since then.

Eve: Yes, we have to ***take the ________ with the smooth***, don't we? We ***can't turn the clock ________***.

Dan: That's for sure. We all have our ________ ***and downs*** in life. But you know I've learnt a lot from that difficult time in my life. I learnt to ***stand on my own ________*** and that we never know what's ***around the ________***, so we should try to ***make the ________ of*** every day.

Eve: Yes, that's very true.

Now check your answers by comparing this page with CONVERSATION 1

Unit 7 - TALKING ABOUT THE PAST - Part 4

In order to become more familiar with these new everyday expressions:

1) **Listen to Conversation 1 again and tick the boxes ☐ next to the expressions as you hear them.**
2) **After the conversation has finished, write in the definitions you can remember. Some have been done as examples.**
3) **Check your answers by turning to page 132.**

☐ takes me back...

☐ get up to .... *.do/be engaged in (something)*...................................

☐ in one piece...

☐ crazy................................*foolish (but exciting)*...................................

☐ burn the candle at both ends....... *have very little sleep (because of too much activity)*..........

☐ take a sickie...

☐ *keep (that) up........................*continue with (that activity)*..............................

☐ *turned upside down ....

☐ get over (it)...

☐ (I'd rather not) go into it..

☐ Fair enough...

☐ strike me as ....*seem/appear to me as (something)*.............................

☐ put this behind me..

☐ get on with (something).............*proceed/continue (with something)*...........................

☐ *haven't looked back..

☐ take the rough with the smooth..

☐ can't turn the clock back...

☐ ups and downs...

☐ *stand on my own feet...

☐ *around the corner..

☐ make the most of ....

LANGUAGE NOTES:

* ***'Keep up'*** can be used before nouns. eg. ***'Keep up*** the good work!' (Continue the good work!) When ***'keep up'*** is used with pronouns, the pronoun goes in the middle of the expression. eg. '***Keep*** it ***up***!', 'I can't ***keep*** this ***up*** for three weeks!'

*When we say something *'has been **turned upside down**'* we usually means *'has been changed in a **negative/disorderly way**'*.

*The expression, *'I haven't looked back',* is always expressed in the negative (***not/never***) but has a positive meaning: *'I have progressed/succeeded /gone forward'*

****'Stand on my own feet'*** can also be expressed as *'Stand on my own **two** feet'*

* We say something is *'**just** around the corner'*, meaning *in the **near** future/ very soon.* eg. 'My birthday is ***just around the corner***.' = 'My birthday is ***very soon***.'

Unit 7 - TALKING ABOUT THE PAST – Part 5

LANGUAGE REVIEW

Complete the sentences, choosing from the everyday expressions which are listed below.
You can use the clues in brackets ( ) at the end of each sentence to help you.
Then complete the crossword using the everyday expressions you have written.
The first one has been done as an example.

keep it up	in one piece	stand on my own feet	get over	make the most of	get on with
ups and downs	~~burn the candle at both ends~~	around the corner	takes me back	sickie	

ACROSS

1) If you ***burn the candle at both ends***, you won't get enough sleep and you could get sick. (have very little sleep because of too much activity)
3) 'I'm pleased to see you are exercising everyday. I hope you _______________'.(continue)
5) She's lucky to be ________________after her terrible car accident. (alive and unharmed)
7) Thanks for your help in the past but I can ______________________ now. (be independent)
9) Christmas is just____________________, so we'd better start preparing. (in the near future)

DOWN

2) 'We've had ________________ in our marriage but we still love each other'. (good and bad experiences)
4) When I look at these old photographs, it ________________ to my time as a student.(makes me remember)
6) It's a great day! Let's _________________ it by having a picnic by the river.(fully use, enjoy)
8) My vacation is over, so I'll have to ______________ my studies now. (proceed with)
10) When I had cancer, I thought I would never _________________it. (recover)
12) Yesterday I took a _________ and relaxed in my garden. (a day off from work)

1 b u r n * t h e * c a n d l e * a t * b o t h * e n d s

Answers, page 119.

Unit 7 - TALKING ABOUT THE PAST – Part 6

FOCUS ON SPOKEN LANGUAGE

A) Talking about the past using 'used to' and 'would'.

When we talk about the past in English, we use different verb tenses to indicate how the past events we are talking about, relate to the present time. In this unit you will see how we use ***'used to'*** or ***'would'*** to indicate ***past habits or activities***.

- We use ***'used to'*** or ***'would'*** to talk about ***a past habit or activity*** which has since been ***discontinued***; to indicate that things have ***changed.*** Look at these examples:
  'I ***used to exercise*** regularly', indicates, 'I don't exercise regularly now.' (Things have changed).
  'When I was single, I ***would*** go to clubs every night', means, 'I don't go to clubs every night now.'
- We use ***'used to'*** to talk about past ***situations*** as well as actions; to indicate how ***a situation has changed***. For example: 'I ***used to be*** single.' (but now I'm married)
  'I ***used to be*** thin.' (but I'm not thin now)
- ***Would*** is used to talk about past habits or actions but is not used to talk about past situations.

1) Read Conversation 1 and note the things that Dan (and his friends) ***used to do***. Complete the following sentences from Conversation 1 on page 72.

We used to____

We used to____

2) Find the things Dan (and his friends) ***would do*** in their younger days. Complete the following sentences. (Note that '***we would***' is spoken as ***we'd***).

We'd____

____….or

we'd ____

3) Does Dan still do those things? ____________________(Answers, page 119)

NOTICE THE PATTERN: used to + (present simple verb) and ***would + (present simple verb)***

Look at these examples and note the pattern.

	(present simple verb)	
I ***used to***	***walk***	regularly but now I catch the bus.
We ***used to***	***do***	some crazy things when we were younger.
I ***would***	***party***	all weekend when I was in my teens but now I stay home on weekends.
We'***d***	***take***	a sickie and go to the beach.

PRACTICE

Think about how your life has changed. Complete the following sentences about your life. Remember we use ***'used to*** *+ present simple verb'* or '***would*** *+ present simple verb'* to talk about past habits and activities which we have **discontinued** now.

When I was younger, I____

Before I left my native country, I __________________________________

See Unit 3, Part 6C (p. 32) for examples of other ways of indicating past time.

Unit 7 - TALKING ABOUT THE PAST – Part 6

FOCUS ON SPOKEN LANGUAGE
B) Pronunciation - Words ending in 'ed'

Listen to the first two lines of Conversation 1(below) and notice the pronunciation of '*ed*' at the end of the words, 'us*ed*' and 'surpris*ed*'. The '*ed*' is ***not*** pronounced as an extra syllable.

Dan: You know, whenever I hear that song, it takes me back to my younger days.........
We us***ed*** to get up to some mischief. I'm surpris***ed*** I'm still in one piece!

The ***ed*** endings of words are pronounced as /**t**/, /**d**/, or /əd/ depending on the sound before ***ed.***

As a general rule:

- /***ed***/ is pronounced as ***t*** after consonant sounds like **s, p, t, th, ch, k, sh.**
  eg. kick***ed*** is pronounced as /kɪk**t**/; missed is pronounced as /mɪs**t**/
- /***ed***/ is pronounced as ***d*** after consonant sounds like **m, n, b, z, v, j, l.**
  eg. hemm***ed*** is pronounced as /hem**d**/; sneez***ed*** is pronounced /sneez**d**/
  (**Note:** surpris**ed** is pronounced /surpri**zd**/ as the **/s/** before **ed** is pronounced **/z/**)

PRACTICE 1
Look at this section from Conversation 1. Put the words in boxes in the correct column below.

Eve: Why, what happened to change things?
Dan: Well, I was at work one day when I received the news that my parents had been killed in a car accident.
Eve: Oh no, that's terrible. I'm so sorry. You haven't talked about that before. It must have been a terrible shock.

Answers, page 120.

words ending in /d/	**words ending with /t/**
happened	

- ***ed*** is pronounced as an extra syllable, /əd/, when added to words which end in ***/d/*** or ***/t/.***
  eg. When ***ed*** is added to the word **visit**, visit***ed*** is pronounced visit***əd.***
  When ***ed*** is added to the word **end**, the word end***ed*** is pronounced as end***əd***

PRACTICE 2

Put the following words in the correct column below. Some have been done as examples.

Answers, page 120.

~~*loved*~~	*waited*	*included*	*looked*	*worked*	*started*	*arrived*	*washed*

ed pronounced as /**d**/	***ed*** pronounced as /**t**/	***ed*** pronounced as /əd/
loved		***waited***

Note: Some past tense verbs are ***spelt*** and ***pronounced*** with a***'t'*** *at the end, rather than* ***'ed'***..
eg. learnt, burnt, spelt, built, wept.

Unit 7 - TALKING ABOUT THE PAST – Part 6

FOCUS ON SPOKEN LANGUAGE

C) Pronunciation /ɪ/ and /e/

In this unit you will practise identifying and pronouncing the sounds, /ɪ/ and /e/
/ɪ/ and /e/ are both ***short*** vowel ***sounds***.
/ɪ/ is the ***symbol*** for the short vowel ***sound*** in the word 'bitter'.
/e/ is the ***symbol*** for the short vowel ***sound*** in the word 'better'.

At the back of this book you will find a PHONEMIC CHART to help you identify and practise the various sounds of English.

Find the following sentence in Conversation 1.
Listen to the pronunciation of the underlined words.

Dan: '..........We can let our experiences in life make us bitter or better'

Words like b*i*tter/b*e*tter, t*i*ll/t*e*ll, p*i*n/p*e*n are sometimes difficult to distinguish from each other as they can sound alike when pronounced in fast speech.
Note that when pronouncing /e/ the mouth is opened wider than /ɪ/.

Practise saying the following sentence, being careful to open your mouth wider for the /e/ sound than the /ɪ/ sound.

'I think Tim is a little bitter because Betty thinks Ben is better at tennis.'

NOTE: There are various ways of ***spelling*** the ***sounds*** /ɪ/ and /e/.

/ɪ/ is a short vowel sound, found in words such as w*i*ll, b***u***sy, p***i***nk, g***y***m, pr***e***tty.
(notice the different ways of spelling the sound /ɪ/).
/e/ is a short vowel sound, found in words such as w***e***t, br***ea***d, s***ai***d.
(notice the different ways of spelling the sound /e/).

English pronunciation can be confusing because words are often ***not*** pronounced the way they are spelt.
A good dictionary will give clear examples of pronunciation and a pronunciation key.
The Pronunciation Key (usually at the front of the dictionary) will show symbols used for English sounds.
If your dictionary is not helpful in showing pronunciation, you should get a better dictionary.

PRACTICE

Use your dictionary to check the pronunciation of each of the following words or ask a native speaker to pronounce them for you. Are the ***underlined vowel sounds*** pronounced as /ɪ / or /e/.

h**ea**d   *busy*   pr**e**tty   *bill*   *big*   *mystery*   s**ai**d   *English*   *egg*

Write the words in the correct column in the chart below. Then check you answers on page 120.

/ɪ/	/e/

UNIT 8

ASKING FOR DIRECTIONS

Unit 8 - ASKING FOR DIRECTIONS – Part 1

Have you ever tried to find your way around an unfamiliar city in peak hour traffic? It can be very confusing! In the following conversation you will hear someone who is lost asking for directions. Before you listen, match the words in the box with their correct meaning listed below. Answers, page 120.

peak hour	bend	overpass	option	avoid	backstreets

choice ____________________
go around/stay away from ____________
bridge over a road/railway ____________

smaller/less important streets __________
a curve in the road _________________
busiest time (for traffic) _____________

Now listen to this conversation in which a driver, who is trying to find his way through the city, asks a service station attendant for directions. The conversation contains everyday expressions which will be explained later in the unit - so don't worry if you don't understand every word. This time you are only listening for a general understanding of the topic. As you listen, tick the correct answers below. (There may be more than one correct answer.) When you have finished you can check your answers on page 120.

1) The driver wants to know the way to

a) Fairmont
b) Fairgrove
c) Highgrove

2) The driver says:

a) he's never been in the area before.
b) he travelled through the area ten years ago.
c) the area has changed a lot.

3) Which of the following ways does the service station attendant suggest:

a) the old road
b) through the backstreets
c) the highway

4) Which way does the driver say he will try?

a) the old road
b) through the backstreets
c) the highway
d) past the hospital

Now we'll look at the everyday expressions used in the conversation - turn to the next page.

Unit 8 - ASKING FOR DIRECTIONS – Part 2A

CONVERSATION 1 (with everyday expressions)

Read this conversation as you listen to the audio cassette. Do you know what the *underlined* words mean? They are colloquial or 'everyday' expressions.

Attendant: ***Are you right there***?

Driver: Actually, I'm ***after*** some directions. Could you tell me the best way to Fairgrove?

Attendant: Sure...now let me think which'd be the best way to go this time of the day. You'll come to ***a bottleneck*** if you go along the highway, so don't go that way.

Driver: Tell me about it! We've been in ***bumper to bumper traffic*** for the last 20***K's.***

Attendant: Yeah, they've been ***doing up*** the road and it's caused more ***hold ups*** than usual.

Driver: You know, I used to travel through this area all the time about ten years ago but it's all changed. They've put in a lot of one way streets and it's completely ***thrown me***.

Attendant: Yeah, it's a bit ***tricky*** around here now but there're a couple of ways you can go other than the highway. You could avoid the ***CBD*** completely by taking the old road. I'll show you on the map you've got there. See here.

Driver: Yes I see...on the other side of the highway.

Attendant: The problem with the old road is that there're quite a few bends and it can be a bit ***hairy;*** especially this time of the day when the ***truckies*** are trying to avoid the peak hour traffic too...and let me tell you, some of them really ***go flat out*** along there

Driver: OK. I'll keep that in mind.

Attendant: Your other option is to go through the backstreets. It's a bit of ***a short cut*** but you won't avoid the traffic completely. Just ***do a U-ie*** here and then take the second on the right back there.

Driver: You mean back there, near the black ***ute***?

Attendant: That's right. Turn right there. Go through two sets of lights. Take the next left and you'll come to ***a dogleg*** in the road. Follow that through, go over the overpass and you'll see signs to Fairgrove. Just ***follow your nose*** from there.

Driver: OK. Thanks very much. Which would be the quickest way?

Attendant: Oh, it's probably ***much of a muchness***. The main thing is to stay off the highway. There's often a ***prang*** this time of day.

Driver: Oh I'll ***be up the creek*** if I'm delayed any longer. I'll try the back streets. Thanks very much for your help.

Attendant: ***No worries***.

Now let's see what these expressions mean - look at the next page.

CONVERSATION 2 (explanation of everyday expressions)

Compare Conversation 1 with Conversation 2 **-You will see that some of the words are different but the meaning is the same in both conversations. Find the underlined words in Conversation 1, then underline the words with the same meaning in Conversation 2. For example: *Are you right there?* (Conversation 1) =*Do you need help?* (Conversation 2)**

Attendant: Do you need help?
Driver: Actually, I'm seeking some directions. Could you tell me the best way to Fairgrove?
Attendant: Sure...now let me think which would be the best way to go this time of the day. You'll come to a crowded section of road if you go along the highway, so don't go that way.
Driver: Tell me about it! We've been in very slow moving traffic for the last 20 kilometres.
Attendant: Yeah, they've been repairing the road and it's caused more delays than usual.
Driver: You know, I used to travel through this area all the time about ten years ago but it's all changed. They've put in a lot of one way streets and it's completely confused me.
Attendant: Yeah, it's a bit difficult around here now but there're a couple of ways you can go other than the highway. You could avoid the central business district completely by taking the old road. I'll show you on the map there. See here.
Driver: Yes I see...on the other side of the highway.
Attendant: The problem with the old road is that there're quite a few bends and it can be a bit dangerous/frightening; especially this time of the day when the truck drivers are trying to avoid the peak hour traffic too and let me tell you; some of them really go very quickly along there.
Driver: OK. I'll keep that in mind.
Attendant: Your other option is to go through the backstreets. It's a bit of a shorter way but you won't avoid the traffic completely. Do a U-turn here (turn around and drive the opposite way) and then take the second on the right back there.
Driver: You mean back there, near the black utility truck*?
Attendant: That's right. Turn right there. Go through two sets of lights. Take the next left and you'll come to a bend in the road. Follow that through, go over the overpass and you'll see signs to Fairgrove. Just go straight ahead from there.
Driver: OK. Thanks very much. Which would be the quickest way?
Attendant: Oh, it's probably almost the same (result). The main thing is to stay off the highway. There's often a car accident this time of day.
Driver: Oh I'll be in trouble/ difficulty if I'm delayed any longer. I'll try the back streets. Thanks very much for your help.
Attendant: You are welcome.

*See illustration page 85.

Now to become familiar with the everyday expressions, practise reading CONVERSATION 1 aloud with a partner.

Unit 8 - ASKING FOR DIRECTIONS – Part 3

Listen to the conversation again and fill in the missing words. You may have to listen more than once. (Don't worry about your spelling as this exercise focuses on listening skills - you can check your spelling later.)

Attendant: ***Are you ______ there***?

Driver: Actually, I'm ______some directions. Could you tell me the best way to Fairgrove?

Attendant: Sure...now let me think which would be the best way to go this time of the day. You'll come to ***a bottleneck*** if you go along the highway, so don't go that way.

Driver: Tell me about it! We've been in ***bumper ____ bumper traffic*** for the last 20***K's.***

Attendant: Yeah, they've been ***doing*** ____ the road and it's caused more ______ ***ups*** than usual.

Driver: You know, I used to travel through this area all the time about ten years ago but it's all changed. They've put in a lot of one way streets and it's completely__________ ***me***.

Attendant: Yeah, it's a bit ***tricky*** around here now but there're a couple of ways you can go other than the highway. You could avoid the ______ completely by taking the old road. I'll show you on the map there. See here.

Driver: Yes I see...on the other side of the highway.

Attendant: The problem with the old road is that there're quite a few bends and it can be a bit _______; especially this time of the day when the ________ are trying to avoid the peak hour traffic too and let me tell you; some of them really ***go ________ out*** along there

Driver: OK. I'll keep that in mind.

Attendant: Your other option is to go through the backstreets. It's a bit of ***a short*** ______but you won't avoid the traffic completely. Just ***do a*** _____ here and then take the second on the right back there.

Driver: You mean back there, near the black ____?

Attendant: That's right. Turn right there. Go through two sets of lights. Take the next left and you'll come to ***a dogleg*** in the road. Follow that through, go over the overpass and you'll see signs to Fairgrove. Just ***follow your*** ______ from there.

Driver: OK. Thanks very much. Which would be the quickest way?

Attendant: Oh, it's probably ***much of a muchness***. The main thing is to stay off the highway. There's often a _______ this time of day.

Driver: Oh, I'll ***be ____ the creek*** if I'm delayed any longer. I'll try the back streets. Thanks very much for your help.

Attendant: ______ ***worries***.

Now check your answers by comparing this page with CONVERSATION 1

Unit 8 - ASKING FOR DIRECTIONS – Part 4

In order to become more familiar with these new everyday expressions:

1) **Listen to Conversation 1 again and tick the boxes ☐ next to the expressions as you hear them.**
2) **After the conversation has finished, write in the definitions you can remember. Some have been done for you as examples.**
3) **Check your answers by turning to page 133.**

☐ Are you right there?..

☐ after ....

☐ *a bottleneck...*a crowded section of road*..............................

☐ bumper to bumper traffic..

☐ k's..

☐ doing up..

☐ hold ups..

☐ thrown me...*confused me*..............................

☐ tricky...*difficult/confusing*..............................

☐ CBD..

☐ hairy..

☐ truckies..

☐ go flat out..

☐ a short cut..

☐ *do a u-ie..

☐ *ute..

☐ a dogleg...*a bend in the road (shaped like a dog's back leg)*..

☐ follow your nose..

☐ much of a muchness..

☐ a prang..

☐ be up the creek..

☐ No worries!...*You are welcome*..............................

a 'ute'

LANGUAGE NOTE:
*'***a bottleneck***' refers to a crowded, congested section of road often caused by the road narrowing or resulting from an intersection of several roads .
*'***Do a U-ie***' is also expressed as '***chuck a U-ie***', though this is more informal.
The driver used the expression, '***Tell me about it!***' It means, '***I agree/I know that***'.

Unit 8 - ASKING FOR DIRECTIONS – Part 5

LANGUAGE REVIEW
Complete the sentences, choosing from the everyday expressions which are listed below.
You can use the clues in brackets ( ) at the end of each sentence to help you.
Then complete the crossword using the everyday expressions you have written.
The first one has been done as an example.

hold ups	~~much of a muchness~~	flat out	up the creek	doing up
truckie	thrown me	short cut	prang	bottleneck
hairy	ute	tricky		

ACROSS

1) You can deliver the order anytime. It's ***much of a muchness*** to me. (It will be the same/ similar result.)
3) Don't go that way! Turn down this road; it's a _______ _______.(shorter way)
5) My son had a ________ in his new car but nobody was hurt. (an accident)
7) I'm taking the train tomorrow. There were lots of ______ ___ on the highway today. (delays)
9) We're _______ ___ our house, so it will look a lot better next time you visit us.(repairing)
11) This game is a bit _________. (difficult)
13) That intersection has become a ______________. They need to put in traffic lights. (crowded section of road)

DOWN

2) They've changed the bus timetable and it has really ________ _____. I missed the bus this morning! (confused me)
4) I want to buy a ______ for work. It'll be good for carrying my tools. (utility truck)
6) My son works as a __________, travelling all over the country. (truck driver)
8) If we get lost, we'll be late and we'll really be __ ____ ________. (in trouble/difficulty)
10) The race was very exciting. The riders were all going ______ _____.(very quickly)
12) The drive down the mountain is really _______It's steep and slippery. (difficult/dangerous)

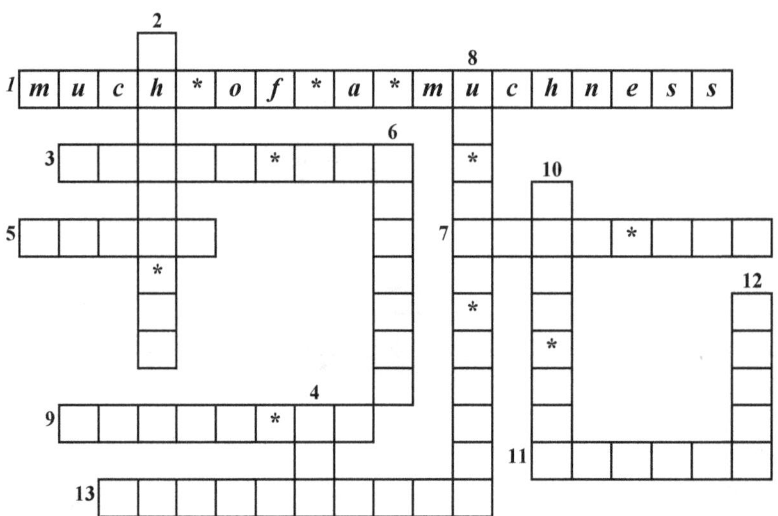

Answers, page 120.

Unit 8 - ASKING FOR DIRECTIONS - Part 6

FOCUS ON SPOKEN LANGUAGE

A) Giving Instructions

When giving instructions or directions in English, we usually begin the instruction with a verb. Read the section below taken from Conversation 1 and notice the pattern used by the service station attendant. The verbs are in ***bold*** at the beginning of each direction.

Notice the pattern used for giving directions. The verb is at the beginning of each direction.

Verb	
Do	a U-ie here and then
take	the second on the right back there..........
Turn	right there.
Go	through two sets of lights.
Take	the next left and you'll come to a dogleg in the road.
Follow	that through,
go	over the overpass and you'll see signs to Fairgrove.
Just **follow**	your nose from there.

In grammar books, this pattern is called an ***'imperative'***.
It is used when we want to be direct with our information.

This pattern is used for giving ***instructions*** on how to do or make something. eg. instructions for games or recipes. The pattern is also used for giving ***commands***, to show authority or when giving ***warnings***. It is also used by parents when ***instructing*** children. Look at the following imperatives. Match the imperative with the situation in which it would most likely be used. One has been done as an example. (Answers: page 121)

IMPERATIVE	**SITUATION**
Mix the sugar and milk together.	instruction for a game
Sit down and be quiet.'	direction
Go up the stairs and then turn right.	command to show authority
Be careful!	instruction for a recipe
Leave the building now!	instruction from parent to small child
Deal five cards to each player.	warning regarding danger

IMPORTANT CULTURAL NOTE:

As mentioned earlier, imperatives are used when we want to be direct when giving information, directions or instructions. However, you should not use this pattern when ***requesting*** service, assistance or information (from shop assistants, service people etc.) as it would be *too direct* and may cause offence.

For example, when ordering coffee at a restaurant you should ***not*** say, 'Give me coffee.'
You should say, ***'Could I have*** coffee, please.' or '***I'd like*** coffee, please.'

(For more practice on using polite language when requesting service, see *Understanding Everyday Australian, Book One, Unit 8*)

Unit 8 - ASKING FOR DIRECTIONS - Part 6

FOCUS ON SPOKEN LANGUAGE
B) Pronunciation (sounds) and Spelling

English spelling and pronunciation can be confusing because words with the same ***sound*** are often ***spelt differently***. In the following section, you will practise using pronunciation ***symbols*** in your dictionary to identify correct pronunciation.

There are only five ***vowel letters*** in the English alphabet. These are ***a, e, i , o, u***. However, there are more ***vowel sounds*** in English than in most other languages, because these vowels ***letters*** can be pronounced as short or long ***sounds***. Also, two vowel sounds can be combined to form a different sound (called a diphthong). For example, the vowel sounds **a** and ɪ can be combined to form the sound /**aɪ**/. Note: /**aɪ**/ is the vowel ***sound*** pronounced in the words, ***eye, why, high.***
Notice the different ways of ***spelling*** the ***sound*** /**aɪ**/.

LISTENING PRACTICE

In the section from Conversation 1 (below) you will see two underlined words: **right** and **time**
How are the words pronounced? Listen to this section of Conversation 1 again.

Attendant: Are you **right** there?
Driver: Actually, I'm after some directions. Could you tell me the best way to Fairgrove?
Attendant: Sure...now let me think which would be the best way this **time** of the day.

You will notice that both words contain the same middle ***sound,*** though the spelling is different. This middle sound is shown in many dictionaries and in the PHONEMIC CHART at the back of this book, as the symbol /**aɪ**/.
For example, if you checked the words **right** and **time** in the Macquarie Dictionary, you would see the symbols /**raɪt**/ and /**taɪm**/ to show you the correct pronunciation.

NOTE: Your dictionary may use a different symbol in place of /**aɪ**/.
Check the words 'time' and 'right' in your dictionary now. What symbol does your dictionary show? Copy the pronunciation symbols from your dictionary to the lines below.

	dictionary symbols		dictionary symbols
time	____________________	right	____________________

PRACTICE
Look at the following words taken from Conversation 1. Check the pronunciation in your dictionary.

	dictionary symbols		dictionary symbols
lights	____________	behind	____________
side	____________	try	____________

Look at the following words. One of the words is pronounced with a different vowel sound to all the others. (One is pronounced with /ɪ/, **the other words are pronounced with** /aɪ/). Check the pronunciation of each word in your dictionary. Which word has a different vowel sound? Answer, page 121.

light	die	buy	aisle	wine	give	dry	height

Unit 8 - ASKING FOR DIRECTIONS - Part 6

FOCUS ON SPOKEN LANGUAGE

Pronunciation and Spelling

C) Words beginning with the letter 'u'

In English, many words beginning with the letter '*u*' (words like *use, unit*), are pronounced with **/ju:/** as the initial sound (like the sound of the word '*you*').

At the back of this book you will find a PHONEMIC CHART to help you identify and practise the various sounds of English.

LISTENING PRACTICE

1) Listen to the following section of Conversation 1 again and notice the pronunciation of ***usual*** and ***used*** to. Can you hear the /ju:/ sound at the beginning of the highlighted words?

Attendant: Yeah, they've been doing up the road and that's caused more hold ups than ***usual.***
Driver: You know, I ***used*** to travel through this area all the time about ten years ago but it's all changed

There are ***two*** other words in Conversation 1, beginning with the letter **u** and pronounced with the same initial sound /ju:/. Can you find them? Write them on the line below.

Answers, page 121.

- Note that some words beginning with the letter '**u**', are pronounced as a short vowel sound, /ʌ /, as in **u**nder, **u**s, **u**p. (These words are ***not*** preceded with the /ju:/ sound).

PRACTICE

2) Check the following words in your dictionary or ask a native speaker to pronounce them.

ute	uniform	umbrella	utensils	useful	union	university

How are they pronounced? One of the words is pronounced with a short vowel sound /ʌ /.

All the other words begin with /ju:/ . Which one is different?

The word ________________ begins with a short vowel sound /ʌ /, so it is different .

Answers, page 121.

UNIT 9

FUTURE PLANS AND POSSIBILITIES

Unit 9 - FUTURE PLANS AND POSSIBILITIES - Part 1

Do you plan for the future or do you just 'let things happen'? In this unit you will hear two friends, Chris and Kerri, talking about what they are going to do when they have finished their tourism course. Before you listen to the conversation, match the following words with the appropriate definition below. Answers, page 121.

philosophy	opportunity	ambitious	goal	eagerly	voluntary (work)

a target for the future ________________ determined to succeed ________________

idea, belief, opinion ________________ unpaid work ________________

happily, with desire ________________ a useful situation________________

Now listen to the conversation and decide which of the following statements are true. (There may be more than one correct answer). You can check your answers on page 121.

1) During the holidays, Chris is going to:

a) learn to fly.

b) visit her family.

c) look for a job.

2) Chris suggests that Kerri should:

a) do some voluntary work.

b) get a job in a shop.

c) see a doctor.

3) Chris thinks:

a) people have to plan if they want to succeed.

b) it isn't important to plan for success.

4) Chris says she is:

a) ambitious.

b) lazy.

c) rich.

Now we'll look at the everyday expressions used in the conversation - turn to the next page.

Unit 9 - FUTURE PLANS AND POSSIBILITIES - Part 2A

CONVERSATION 1 (with everyday expressions)

Read this conversation as you listen to the audio cassette. Do you know what the *underlined* words mean? They are colloquial or 'everyday' expressions.

Chris: Only one week left till the end of our course. I can't believe the year's ***just about*** over.

Kerri: Me neither.

Chris: What are you doing in the holidays? Anything exciting?

Kerri: No, not really. I suppose, I'll just ***play it by ear***. What about you, Chris? Any plans?

Chris: Yes, I'm going to visit my family in the country for a week. I'm flying out next Wednesday. I haven't seen them for a while so I'm really ***looking forward to*** it. And then, when I come back, I'm going to look for a job.... as a tour guide if possible.

Kerri: I guess, I'll look for a job too but I must say, I'm a bit ***half hearted about*** it.

Chris: Why's that?

Kerri: Well, ***let's face it***, ***every Tom, Dick and Harry*** will be looking for work this time of year. And the other problem is, employers usually want experienced staff, not students straight out of college.

Chris: True, so why not get some experience in the holidays by doing some voluntary work? That's what I'm going to do if I don't get a job ***straight away.***

Kerri: Mm. I suppose it'd be better than sitting around, ***twiddling my thumbs***. But I'm not ***wrapped in the idea*** of working for nothing.

Chris: Well, the way I look at it, you'd be ***killing two birds with one stone***. It'd be ***paving the way*** for future work and helping someone at the same time. And ***you never know*** - it may lead to a job ***down the track***.

Kerri: You know, I ***have to hand it to you***, Chris. You seem to ***have it all worked out***. I'm the sort of person who hopes opportunities'll ***turn up*** ***out of the blue***. I don't plan ahead like you.

Chris: Well, as far as I'm concerned, you have to plan if you want be successful - if you just wait for something to turn up, it may never happen. I believe we have to ***set our sights on*** something we want and then ***go for it***! I suppose I'm ambitious but I believe we have to create our own opportunities.

Kerri: Well, I can see you're going to ***go places***, that's for sure. You have a good philosophy on life. Maybe I should ***get my act together*** and set some goals too..... Look, I'm going to get a cup of coffee. Would you like one?

Chris: That sounds like a very good idea. I'll just get my bag.

Now let's see what these expressions mean - look at the next page.

CONVERSATION 2 (explanation of everyday expressions)

Compare Conversation 1 with Conversation 2 **-You will see that some of the words are different but the meaning is the same in both conversations. Find the underlined words in Conversation 1, then underline the words with the same meaning in Conversation 2. For example: *just about* (Conversation 1) = *almost* (Conversation 2)**

Chris: (There is) only one week till the end of our course. I can't believe the year's almost over.

Kerri: Me neither.

Chris: What are you doing in the holidays? Anything exciting?

Kerri: No, not really. I suppose, I'll just wait and see what happens (I don't have a plan). What about you, Chris? Any plans?

Chris: Yes, I'm going to visit my family in the country for a week. I'm flying out next Wednesday. I haven't seen them for a while so I'm really eagerly awaiting it. And then, when I come back, I'm going to look for a job.... as a tour guide if possible.

Kerri: I guess I'll look for a job too but I must say, I'm a bit disinterested/only half interested in it.

Chris: Why's that?

Kerri: Well, we must be realistic, a lot of ordinary people will be looking for work this time of year. And the other problem is, employers usually want experienced staff, not students (who are) straight out of college.

Chris: True, so why not get some experience in the holidays by doing some voluntary work? That's what I'm going to do if I don't get a job immediately.

Kerri: Mm. I suppose it'd be better than sitting around, doing nothing. But I'm not happy about the idea of working for nothing.

Chris: Well, the way I look at it, you'd be achieving two things with one action. It'd be preparing the way for future work and helping someone at the same time. And there is a possibility- it may lead to a job in the future.

Kerri: You know, I have to admire/congratulate you, Chris. You seem to have everything planned and organised. I'm the sort of person who hopes opportunities'll arrive/happen unexpectedly (without planning). I don't plan ahead like you.

Chris: Well, as far as I'm concerned, you have to plan if you want be successful - if you just wait for something to turn up, it may never happen. I believe we have to decide and aim for something we want and then strive/try hard (to get what we want!) I suppose I'm ambitious but I believe we have to create our own opportunities.

Kerri: Well, I can see you're going to be successful, that's for sure. You have a good philosophy on life. Maybe I should get organised and set some goals too..... Look, I'm going to get a cup of coffee. Would you like one?

Chris: That sounds like a very good idea. I'll just get my bag.

Now to become familiar with the everyday expressions, practise reading CONVERSATION 1 aloud with a partner.

Unit 9 - FUTURE PLANS AND POSSIBILITIES – Part 3

Listen to the conversation again and fill in the missing words. You may have to listen more than once. (Don't worry about your spelling as this exercise focuses on listening skills - you can check your spelling later.)

Chris: Only one week left till the end of our course. I can't believe the year's ***just*** ________ over.

Kerri: Me neither.

Chris: What are you doing in the holidays? Anything exciting?

Kerri: No, not really. I suppose, I'll just ***play it by*** ________. What about you, Chris? Any plans?

Chris: Yes, I'm going to visit my family in the country for a week. I'm flying out next Wednesday. I haven't seen them for a while so I'm really ***looking*** ________ ***to*** it. And then, when I come back, I'm going to look for a job.... as a tour guide if possible.

Kerri: I guess, I'll look for a job too but I must say, I'm a bit ________ ***hearted about*** it.

Chris: Why's that?

Kerri: Well, ***let's*** ________ ***it***, ***every Tom, Dick and Harry*** will be looking for work this time of year. And the other problem is, employers usually want experienced staff, not students straight out of college.

Chris: True, so why not get some experience in the holidays by doing some voluntary work? That's what I'm going to do if I don't get a job ________ ***away.***

Kerri: Mm. I suppose it'd be better than sitting around, ***twiddling my*** ________. But I'm not ***wrapped in the idea*** of working for nothing.

Chris: Well, the way I look at it, you'd ***be killing two*** ________ ***with one stone***. It'd be ***paving the way*** for future work and helping someone at the same time. And ***you never know*** - it may lead to a job ***down the*** ________.

Kerri: You know, I ***have to*** ________ ***it to you***, Chris. You seem to ***have it all worked*** ________. I'm the sort of person who hopes opportunities'll ***turn up out of the*** ________. I don't plan ahead like you.

Chris: Well, as far as I'm concerned, you have to plan if you want be successful - if you just wait for something to turn up, it may never happen. I believe we have to ***set our*** ________ ***on*** something we want and then ________ ***for it***! I suppose I'm ambitious but I believe we have to create our own opportunities.

Kerri: Well, I can see you're going to ***go*** ________, that's for sure. You have a good philosophy on life. Maybe I should ***get my*** ________ ***together*** and set some goals too..... Look, I'm going to get a cup of coffee. Would you like one?

Chris: That sounds like a very good idea. I'll just get my bag.

Now check your answers by comparing this page with Conversation 1.

Unit 9 - FUTURE PLANS AND POSSIBILITIES – Part 4

In order to become more familiar with these new everyday expressions:

1) **Listen to Conversation 1 again and tick the boxes ☐ next to the expressions as you hear them.**
2) **After the conversation has finished, write in the definitions you can remember. Some have been done for you as examples.**
3) **Check your answers by turning to page 134.**

☐ just about..

☐ play it by ear..

☐ looking forward to..

☐ half hearted (about).................*disinterested (only half interested)*...........................

☐ let's face it..

☐ every Tom, Dick and Harry..

☐ straight away..

☐ twiddling my thumbs..

☐ wrapped in the idea.................*happy about the idea*...

☐ killing two birds with one stone....*achieving two things/results with one action*..............

☐ paving the way..

☐ you never know.....................*there is a possibility* ....

☐ down the track ....

☐ have to hand it to (you)..

☐ have it all worked out..

☐ turn up............................... *arrive/occur/happen* ....

☐ out of the blue..........................*unexpectedly/without planning*................................

☐ set (our) sights on ....

☐ go for it!..

☐ go places..

☐ get my act together..

LANGUAGE NOTE: The expression '***turn up***' can be used for ***people, events*** and ***things***.
For example:

'What time did Tom ***turn up***?'	= 'What time did Tom ***arrive***?'
'Don't worry. Something will ***turn up***.'	= 'Don't worry. Something will ***happen*** (to help this problem).'
'Don't worry. Your purse will ***turn up***.'	= 'Don't worry. Your purse will ***be found***.'

Unit 9 - FUTURE PLANS AND POSSIBILITIES – Part 5

LANGUAGE REVIEW

Complete the sentences, choosing from the everyday expressions which are listed below.
You can use the clues in brackets ( ) at the end of each sentence to help you.
Then complete the crossword using the everyday expressions you have written.
The first one has been done as an example.

straight away	play it by ear	the blue	~~get my act together~~	you never know	face it
looking forward to	pave the way	just about	go places	wrapped in the idea	

ACROSS

1) I should ***get my act together*** and start saving to buy a house. (get organised)
3) We haven't planned anything for New Year's Eve. We'll just____________________.(see what happens)
5) This course will______________for the job I really want. (prepare the way)
7) We have to __________. Our business isn't doing well. (be realistic)
9) We heard the news and we came _____________. (immediately)
11) I think you should go to the dance tonight. _________________ - you may meet your perfect partner. (there is a possibility)

DOWN

2) He is going to __________. Look how well he is progressing already. (be successful)
4) I have _______________ finished painting the house. (almost)
6) I'm ___________________ of getting married in Springtime. (happy about)
8) We are ______________________seeing their new baby. (eagerly awaiting)
10) He was very healthy until suddenly, out of_________, he had a heart attack. (unexpectedly)

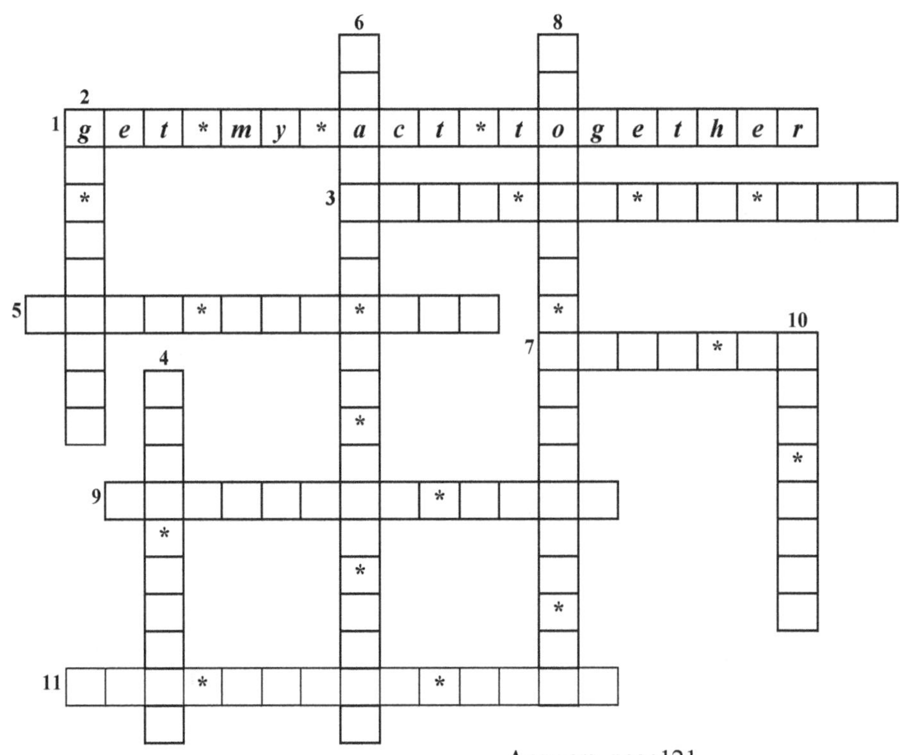

Answers, page121.

Unit 9 - FUTURE PLANS AND POSSIBILITIES – Part 6

FOCUS ON SPOKEN LANGUAGE - ***Talking about the future***

There are several verb forms used to talk about the future in English.

- We talk about our ***plans and intentions*** - this will be examined in section **A** and **B**.
- We ***predict what we think will happen*** - this will be examined in section **C**.
- We talk about ***definite future arrangements*** - section **D**.

In section **A** and **B** we examine two verb forms which were used by the speakers in Conversation 1 to talk about their ***plans and intentions***.

- ***will*** + verb eg. I'***ll*** just ***play*** it by ear. (I ***will*** is usually contracted to I ***'ll***).
- ***am going to*** +verb eg. I'***m going to visit*** my family in the country for a week.

Talking about future plans and intentions

A) We use ***will*** when we are deciding at the moment of speaking what we will do.
For this reason, ***I'll*** is often used with expressions such as '*I think*', '*I suppose*', or '*I guess*'.
The following sentences have been taken from Conversation 1.
In each example, the speaker is ***making a decision at the time of speaking***.

PRACTICE 1

Find the sentences in Conversation 1, then complete each sentence with ***will + verb***.

Kerri: I suppose, I'_______just _________ it by ear.

Kerri: I guess, I______________ for a job too.

Chris: I'____________just ______ my bag. Answers, page 122.

In each of the above sentences, the speakers are making a decision at the moment of speaking. They had not decided or planned their action before speaking.

Notice the pattern:

	will +	*verb (present simple)*
I suppose	I'***ll*** (just)	***play*** it by ear.
I guess	I'***ll***	***look*** for a job too.
	I'***ll*** (just)	***get*** my bag.

PRACTICE 2

Complete the following conversations. Remember, the second speakers are making their decision at *the moment of speaking*, so use ***will + verb***. Answers, page 122.

1st Speaker: This box is very heavy! 2nd Speaker: Wait a minute. I ___________you.
1st Speaker: Oh, I forgot to post this letter! 2nd Speaker: Don't worry. I ____________it later.

B) We use ***going to*** when we talk about things that ***have been decided or planned before the moment of speaking***. The following sentences have been taken from Conversation 1. In each example, the speaker had made their decision ***before*** the time of speaking.
Find the sentences in Conversation 1, then complete each sentence with ***am*** + ***going to*** + ***verb***.

Answers, page 122.

am +	*going to* +	*verb (present simple)*	
Yes, I'***m***	***going to***	***visit***	my family in the country for a week.
...... I'***m***			for a job.......as a tour guide if possible.
That's what I'***m***			if I don't get a job straight away.
Look, I'			a cup of coffee. Would you like one?

NOTE: Because ***going to*** + ***verb*** suggests *premeditated intention*, it is ***not*** usually used with expressions such as, '*I think*', '*I guess*' or '*I suppose*' when talking about plans.
For example, we would ***not*** say, '*I think* I'm going to get a cup of coffee'.

Unit 9 - FUTURE PLANS AND POSSIBILITIES – Part 6

FOCUS ON SPOKEN LANGUAGE - ***Talking about the Future (continued)***

REMEMBER

- We use ***will*** when the speaker decides/plans ***at the time of speaking.***
- We use ***going to*** when the decision was made ***before*** the time of speaking.

PRACTICE

Complete the following conversation about future plans using ***will*** or ***going to.***

Sue: What are you going to do on Saturday?

Pat: I'm not sure yet. I think I__________ stay home and finish my homework.

Sue: Jenni and I are ___________go to the beach. Would you like to come?

Pat: Yes. That sounds great! I _____finish my homework on Sunday instead.

Sue: OK. We're ______________catch the bus at 8 a.m.

Pat: OK. I ______meet you at the bus stop then. What are you _________take for lunch?

Sue: I'm not sure yet. I guess I _________just take some fruit and a sandwich.

(Answers: page 122)

C) ***Making Predictions***

When we predict (say what we think will happen in the future), we can use ***will or going to.***

For example: 'It'***s going to rain*** tomorrow.' *or* 'I think, it ***will rain*** tomorrow.'

'I'***m going to have*** a big phone bill this month.' *or* 'I***'ll have*** a big phone bill this month.'

'Tom ***is going to do*** *well* in the competition.' *or* 'Tom ***will do*** *well* in the competition.'

In Conversation 1, Kerri makes a prediction about Chris.
Read Conversation 1 again, find and complete the following sentence.

Kerri: ......I can see_______________________***go places.*** Answers, page 122

PRACTICE

Look at the picture. Make a prediction about what is going to happen in the game of cricket.
(The person with the bat is called the batter. The person behind the wicket is the wicket keeper).
Write some sentences using ***will*** or ***is going to***.

____

____

Make a prediction about your next electricity bill. How much do you think it will be?

____

Unit 9 - FUTURE PLANS AND POSSIBILITIES – Part 6

FOCUS ON SPOKEN LANGUAGE

D) Talking about definite future arrangements

When we talk about ***definite plans that have already been arranged***, we often use the present progressive tense (also called the present continuous tense). The ***present progressive tense*** is formed with ***am / are / is / + ing.*** We use it to talk about plans that have been confirmed.

Look at this example from Conversation 1.

Chris: 'Yes, I'm going to visit my family in the country for a week. I'***m flying*** out next Wednesday.'

Chris uses the *present progressive tense (am flying)* because her plan is definite.
It is about a *present*, as well as *future* situation - she already has her airline ticket.

Look at the following conversation about future plans and happenings.

Lin: 'What ***are*** you ***doing*** at Christmas this year? ***Are*** you ***going*** away on holidays?'
Ann: 'Not this year. I***'m having**** a baby in January, so ***we're staying*** at home this Christmas.'

Ann used the *present progressive tense* (*am having*) because there is *present* evidence of her baby's future birth.
Ann may also say, 'I'm ***going to have*** a baby in January, so we're ***going to stay*** at home this Christmas.'

Note: Native speakers do ***not*** usually say,
'I'***ll*** have a baby in January, so we'***ll*** stay at home this Christmas.'

*The verb ***'have'*** is used in a variety of ways in English. See Unit 10, Part 6C for details.

PRACTICE

Do you have any definite arrangements for next week? (eg. appointments, visits, classes?)
Complete the sentence using ***am + ...ing....***

Next week, I____.

REVISION AND PRACTICE - Talking about the future

Complete the following conversation by writing the correct verb in the spaces.

Use ***will, am/is going to,*** or ***am/is ...ing (present progressive tense)*** with the verb in brackets.
The first one has been done as an example.
You can check your answers on page 122.

Rai: What ***are*** you ***going to do*** (*do*) while you're on holidays next week?
Jan: I____________(*stay*) with my sister, Kate, and help her look after her two small sons.
Rai: Why? Is she sick?
Jan: No. She____________(*have*) another baby.
Rai: Really? In that case, I__________(*call*) her on the phone tonight and congratulate her.
Jan: Oh good! I'm sure, she__________(*be*) happy to hear from you.
Rai: In fact, I think I_________(*go*) to the shops tomorrow and buy a present for her. Any ideas?
Jan: Well, the weather_____________(*be*) hot when the baby's born...
Rai: I know! I__________(*buy*) her a fan!

UNIT 10

HAVING DINNER WITH FRIENDS

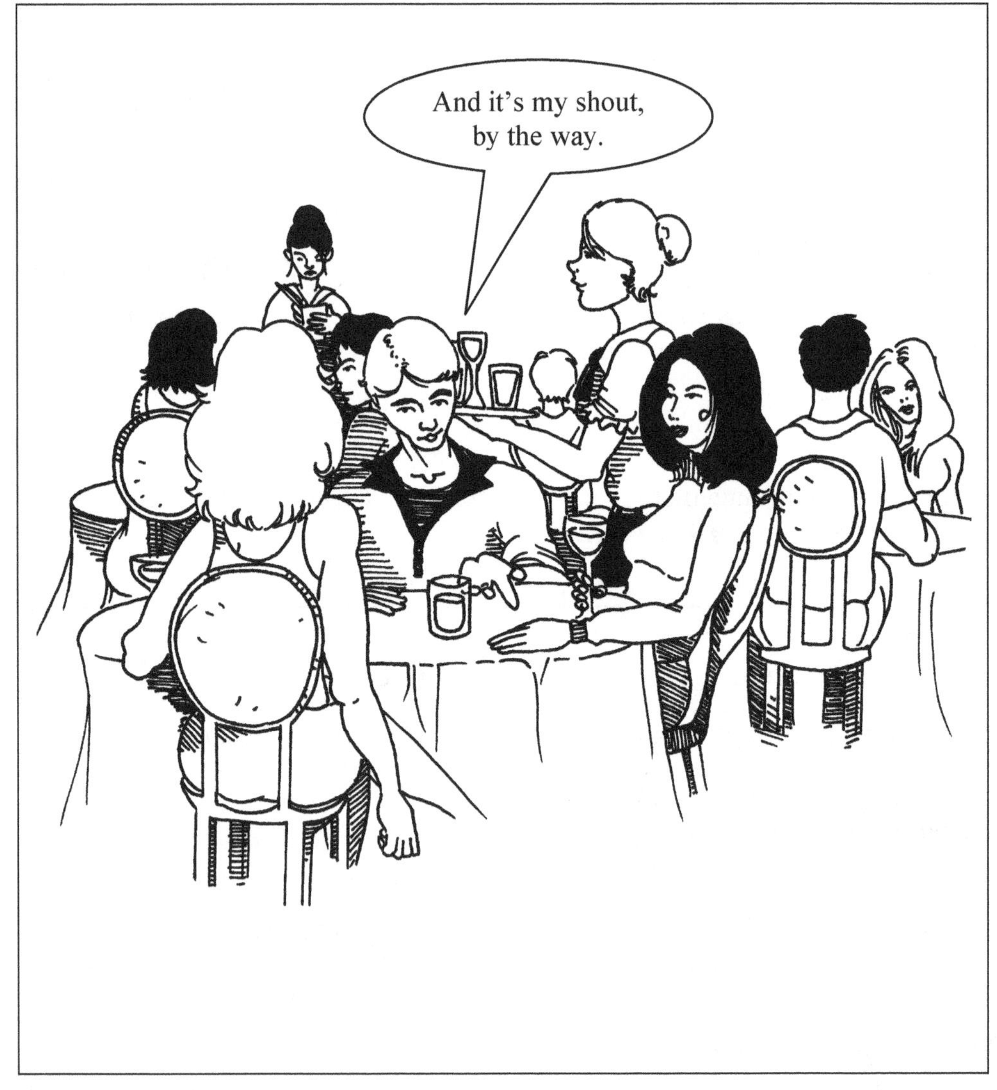

Unit 10 - HAVING DINNER WITH FRIENDS - Part 1

In this Unit you will listen to a conversation between friends, Mal, Lee and Julie, who are having dinner together. The conversation contains 'everyday' expressions which will be explained later in the unit - so don't worry if you don't understand every word.

A) Before you listen, match the words in the box with the meanings listed below.

a la carte	buffet	cafeteria

a place where customers collect their meal on a tray from a counter ____________________

a meal in which customers select from a variety of displayed food ____________________

a restaurant where a variety of meals may be ordered from a menu ____________________

Answer, page 122.

B) As you listen to the conversation, decide which of the above expressions best describes the type of meal the friends are having.________________________________

As you listen again, tick the correct answers below. (There may be more than one correct answer.) When you have finished you can check your answers on page 122.

1) How many of the friends are going to have prawns?

a) none

b) one

c) two

d) three

2) What are the ladies going to drink?

a) orange juice

b) wine

c) beer

3) When Julie asked about the movie:

a) both friends said it was very funny

b) one friend said it was OK but the other friend thought it was very funny.

Now we'll look at the everyday expressions used in the conversation - turn to the next page.

Unit 10 - HAVING DINNER WITH FRIENDS - Part 2A

CONVERSATION 1 (with everyday expressions)

Read this conversation as you listen to the audio recording. Do you know what the *underlined* words mean? They are colloquial or 'everyday' expressions.

Mal: Well, I know what I'm going to have....What about you two?

Lee: It's ***a toss up*** between the roast beef and the pork chops. What've you decided on?

Mal: I'm going to have the prawns in chilli sauce. It was delicious last time.

Lee: Mm..I love prawns too but spicy food ***doesn't agree with me***. So I won't have that.

Julie: Me neither. I'm going to ***steer clear of*** prawns from now on. I had some that were ***off*** a few months ago and I ***can't stand*** them now.

Lee: Really? You didn't have them here, did you?

Julie: No, no. It was at the seafood restaurant on North Street. When I told them about it they offered me a meal ***on the house*** but I haven't been back since.

Lee: Well, ***I don't blame you.*** I heard that place isn't much good anyway. Now what'll I have.....I think, I'll ***go for*** the roast.

Julie: Me too. The roast beef is always good here. And what about something to drink? Would you like some wine?

Lee: That sounds like a good idea.

Mal: I'm going to have a beer. And it's ***my shout***, by the way. You paid for the last ***round***.

Julie: Oh OK, thanks Mal. Would you like a bottle of red or white, Lee?

Lee: ***I'm easy***; you decide.... ***on second thoughts***, maybe we should buy it by the glass. I don't want to have too much to drink tonight. We're having an important meeting at work tomorrow, so I don't want ***a hangover.***

Julie: That's OK. Don't worry. I'll ***polish off*** what you can't drink... So tell me about the movie you went to see last night.

Mal: Oh I thought it was ***a scream***. It was ***a send up*** about marriage and it was so funny. You weren't very ***taken with*** it though were you, Lee?

Lee: Oh it was OK. It was a bit ***over the top***, that's all. A bit ***far-fetched,*** you know.

Mal: Yes but that's what made it so funny.

Julie: It looks like I'll have to go and ***check it out*** myself.

Mal: Here comes the waiter. What are we all having again?

Now let's see what these expressions mean - look at the next page.

CONVERSATION 2 (explanation of everyday expressions)

Compare Conversation 1 with Conversation 2 **-You will see that some of the words are different but the meaning is the same in both conversations. Find the underlined words in Conversation 1, then underline the words with the same meaning in Conversation 2. For example: a toss up (Conversation 1) = a choice/decision (Conversation 2)**

Mal: Well, I know what I'm going to have....What about you two?

Lee: It's a choice/decision between the roast beef and the pork chops. What've you decided on?

Mal: I'm going to have the prawns in chilli sauce. It was delicious last time.

Lee: Mm..I love prawns too but spicy food isn't good for my health. So I won't have that.

Julie: Me neither. I'm going to avoid prawns from now on. I had some that were bad/stale a few months ago and I dislike them (very much) now.

Lee: Really? You didn't have them here, did you?

Julie: No, no. It was at the seafood restaurant on North Street. When I told them about it, they offered me a meal at no cost/ free (at the management's expense) but I haven't been back since.

Lee: Well, I understand your decision. I heard that place isn't much good, anyway. Now what'll I have.....I think, I'll choose /have the roast.

Julie: Me too. The roast beef is always good here. And what about something to drink? Would you like some wine?

Lee: That sounds like a good idea.

Mal: I'm going to have a beer. And it's my treat (I will pay for you), by the way. You paid for the last set of drinks (one for each member).

Julie: Oh OK, thanks Mal. Would you like a bottle of red or white, Lee?

Lee: I'll be happy with either choice; you decide...after thinking more about it, maybe we should buy it by the glass. I don't want to have too much to drink tonight. We're having an important meeting at work tomorrow, so I don't want a headache etc. caused by too much alcohol.

Julie: That's OK. Don't worry. I'll finish what you can't drink... So tell me about the movie you went to see last night.

Mal: Oh I thought it was a very funny (thing). It was an entertaining mimic (joke) about marriage and it was so funny. You weren't very impressed with it though were you, Lee?

Lee: Oh it was OK. It was a bit exaggerated /extreme, that's all. A bit unbelievable you know.

Mal: Yes but that's what made it so funny.

Julie: It looks like I'll have to go and see/ investigate it myself.

Mal: Here comes the waiter. What are we all having again?

Now to become familiar with the everyday expressions, practise reading CONVERSATION 1 aloud with a partner.

Unit 10 - HAVING DINNER WITH FRIENDS - Part 3

Listen to the conversation again and fill in the missing words. You may have to listen more than once. (Don't worry about your spelling as this exercise focuses on listening skills - you can check your spelling later.)

Mal: Well, I know what I'm going to have....What about you two?

Lee: It's ***a toss*** ______ between the roast beef and the pork chops. What've you decided on?

Mal: I'm going to have the prawns in chilli sauce. It was delicious last time.

Lee: Mm..I love prawns too but spicy food ***doesn't*** ______ ***with me***. So I won't have that.

Julie: Me neither. I'm going to ***steer*** ______ ***of*** prawns from now on. I had some that were ***off*** a few months ago and I ***can't*** ______ them now.

Lee: Really? You didn't have them here, did you?

Julie: No, no. It was at the seafood restaurant on North Street. When I told them about it they offered me a meal ***on the*** ______ but I haven't been back since.

Lee: Well, ***I don't blame you.*** I heard that place isn't much good anyway. Now what'll I have.....I think, I'll ______ ***for*** the roast.

Julie: Me too. The roast beef is always good here. And what about something to drink? Would you like some wine?

Lee: That sounds like a good idea.

Mal: I'm going to have a beer. And it's ***my*** ______, by the way. You paid for the last ______.

Julie: Oh OK, thanks Mal. Would you like a bottle of red or white, Lee?

Lee: ***I'm*** ______; you decide....***on*** ______ ***thoughts***, maybe we should buy it by the glass. I don't want to have too much to drink tonight. We're having an important meeting at work tomorrow, so I don't want ***a hangover.***

Julie: That's OK. Don't worry. I'll ***polish*** ______ what you can't drink... So tell me about the movie you went to see last night.

Mal: Oh I thought it was ***a*** ______. It was ***a*** ______ ***up*** about marriage and it was so funny. You weren't very ***taken with*** it though were you, Lee?

Lee: Oh it was OK. It was a bit ***over the*** ______, that's all. A bit ______***-fetched,*** you know.

Mal: Yes but that's what made it so funny.

Julie: It looks like I'll have to go and ***check it*** ______ myself.

Mal: Here comes the waiter. What are we all having again?

Now check your answers by comparing this page with Conversation 1.

Unit 10 - HAVING DINNER WITH FRIENDS - Part 4

In order to become more familiar with these new everyday expressions:

1) **Listen to Conversation 1 again and tick the boxes ☐ next to the expressions as you hear them.**
2) **After the conversation has finished, write in the definitions you can remember. Some have been done for you as examples.**
3) **Check your answers by turning to page 135.**

☐ a toss up...

☐ doesn't agree with me..

☐ steer clear of...

☐ off...

☐ can't stand...

☐ on the house...

☐ I don't blame you........................*I understand your decision*..................................

☐ go for....................................*choose/ have*...

☐ my shout..................................*it's my treat/ I will pay for you*...............................

☐ round......................................*set of drinks (one for each member)*.......................

☐ I'm easy...

☐ on second thoughts..

☐ a hangover..

☐ polish off..

☐ a scream...

☐ a send up..

☐ taken with.............................*impressed with*..

☐ over the top ....

☐ far-fetched...

☐ check it out...

CULTURAL NOTE:

When refusing food which has been offered to us, it may be offensive to refuse by saying, 'I don't like it'. However, to say that a particular food '***doesn't agree with me***', (meaning that the food 'will cause a disagreeable reaction on my health') should not cause offence as it is a health issue rather than a rejection of the food. For example, I may like milk but be unable to eat food containing milk because it '***doesn't agree with***' my health.

Unit 10 - HAVING DINNER WITH FRIENDS - Part 5

LANGUAGE REVIEW

Complete the sentences, choosing from the everyday expressions which are listed below. You can use the clues in brackets ( ) at the end of each sentence to help you. Then complete the crossword using the everyday expressions you have written. One has been done as an example.

off	steer clear of	taken with	far-fetched	over the top	polished off
hangover	a scream	toss up	~~on second thoughts~~	on the house	

ACROSS

1) I'll finish my essay today.....***on second thoughts***, I won't have a chance to finish it till tomorrow. (after thinking about it more)
3) I'm going to ________________ that shopping centre. It's always too busy. (avoid)
5) The story he told us was too________________. I didn't believe a word of it. (unbelievable)
7) It's opening night at the new restaurant, so to celebrate, the drinks are______________.(free)
9) I don't think you should cook that fish. It smells _______. (bad/ stale)
11) I don't know which hat to buy. It's a ____________between the red or green one. (choice)

DOWN

2) We've heard that the show is ____________ so we've booked to see it. (very funny)
4) The costumes in the parade were ________________in my opinion. (exaggerated/ extreme)
6) Who ________________ all the cake? There's none left! (finished)
8) If you keep drinking, you'll have a __________tomorrow. (headache from too much alcohol)
10) She's very ______________her new teacher. She said he is very clever. (impressed by)

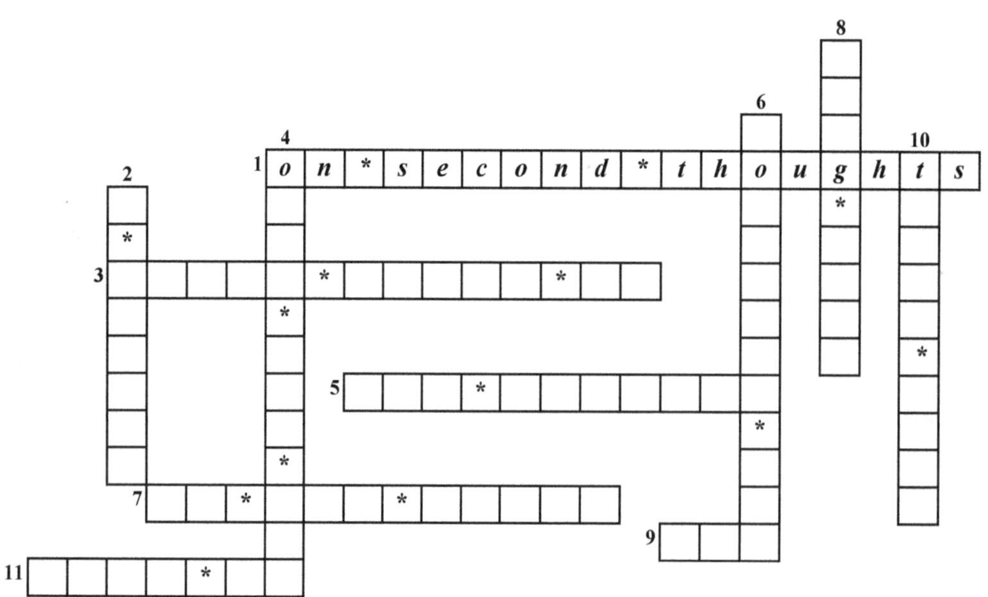

Answers, page 123.

Unit 10 - HAVING DINNER WITH FRIENDS - Part 6

FOCUS ON SPOKEN LANGUAGE

A) Pronunciation and Spelling (Different sounds of the letter 'o').

English pronunciation can be confusing because words containing the *same vowel **letter*** are often pronounced with a *different* **sound.** For example, in the words, ***not***, ***nor***, ***note***, the letter '**o**' is pronounced differently.
In the first word '***not***', the letter '**o**' is pronounced as a short sound represented by the symbol /ɒ/.
In the second word, '***nor***', the letter '**o**' has a long sound /ɔ:/.
In the third word, '***note***', the letter '**o**' is pronounced as a diphthong (two vowel sounds together), represented by /əʊ/.

/ɒ/ /ɔ:/ /əʊ/
The sounds /ɒ/, /ɔ:/, /əʊ/ can all be spelt with the letter '**o**', as in the examples (n**o**t, n**o**r, n**o**te), as well as a variety of other spellings. For example:

/ɒ/ is a short vowel sound, found in words such as n**o**t, wh**a**t, **o**ff
/ɔ:/ is a long vowel sound, found in words such as pr**aw**n, m**ore**, f**ou**r, w**ar**, fl**oo**r
/əʊ/ is a long vowel sound consisting of two vowel sounds, found in words like g**o**, sl**ow**, t**oa**st.

In this unit you will practise distinguishing between the three sounds /ɒ/, /ɔ:/, /əʊ/.

Carefully listen to the following section from Conversation 1 on your audio cassette.
Notice the way the speakers pronounce the words in boxes.
Decide which words are pronounced with a short vowel sound /ɒ/, which have a long vowel sound /ɔ:/, and which are pronounced with a long diphthong sound /əʊ/.

Lee: It's a [toss] up between the [roast] beef and the [pork] [chops]. What've you decided on?
Mal: I'm going to have the [prawns] in chilli [sauce]. It was delicious last time.
Lee: Mm...I love prawns too but spicy food doesn't agree with me. So I [won't] have that.
Julie: Me neither. I'm going to steer clear of prawns from now [on]. I had some that were [off] a few months ago and I can't stand them now.
Lee: Really? You didn't have them here, did you?
Julie: No, [no]. It was at the seafood restaurant on [North] Street. When I [told] them about it they offered me a meal on the house but I haven't been back since.
Lee: Well, I [don't] blame you. I heard that place isn't much good anyway. Now what'll I have.....I think, I'll [go] for the [roast].

Write the words in the correct column below. Some have been done as examples.

words with /ɒ/ (short vowel sound)	words with /ɔ:/ (long vowel sound)	words with /əʊ/ (diphthong sound)
toss	**pork**	**roast**

Answers, page 123.

At the back of this book you will find a PHONEMIC CHART to help you identify and practise the various sounds of English.

Unit 10 - HAVING DINNER WITH FRIENDS - Part 6

FOCUS ON SPOKEN LANGUAGE

B) Using 'too'/'neither' to agree with another person's choice/opinion/decision

1) Me neither. (Note: ***neither*** can be pronounced as /ni:ðə/ or /naɪðə/).

In Conversation 1, Julie agreed with Lee's decision ***not*** to order prawns for dinner. Read the Conversation again (page 102), and note the expression she used to agree with Lee's choice ***not*** to have prawns. Complete the conversation by writing the expression Julie used in the space below.

> Lee: Mm...I love prawns too but spicy food doesn't agree with me. So I ***won't*** have that.
> Julie: _______________. I'm going to steer clear of prawns from now on. I had some that were off a few months ago and I can't stand them now.
>
> Answer, page 123.

When used in this way, '***neither***' means '***also not***'.
In spoken language we can use, '***Me neither***'***,*** when we want to ***agree with a <u>negative</u> statement.*** For example, 'I ca***n't*** speak French.' - 'Me ***neither***'. This means, 'I ***<u>also</u> can <u>not</u>*** speak French.' ('***Neither can I***' and '***Nor can I***' have the same meaning).

Look at the following examples:

Lee's choice/opinion	Julie thinks the same as Lee.	Mal thinks differently to Lee.
I ***won't*** have prawns.	Me ***neither***. (also ***Neither will I.***)	I will (have prawns).
I***'m not*** going to have beer.	Me ***neither***. (also ***Neither am I.***)	I am (going to have beer).
I ***didn't*** like the movie.	Me ***neither***. (also ***Neither did I.***)	I did (enjoy the movie).

2) Me too.

Later in the conversation, Julie ***agreed*** with Lee's decision about having roast beef for dinner. What did she say? Check Conversation 1 and fill in the missing expression.

> Lee: Now what'll I have…..I think, I'***ll*** go for the roast.
> Julie:_______________. The roast beef is always good here.

In spoken language we use, '***Me too***'***,*** when we want to ***agree with a <u>positive</u> statement.*** For example, 'I'***m*** studying English'. - 'Me ***too***.' (This means: I ***am also*** studying English.) ('***So am I.***' has the same meaning).

PRACTICE:

3) Look at the following conversation about food preferences.
Fill in the missing words, using ***too*** and ***neither***.

Bev: I ***don't*** eat dairy products much these days. They don't agree with me.
Noni: Me ____________. I'm allergic to milk.
Bev: I ***can't*** stand cheese.
Noni: Me__________ . It makes me feel sick.
Bev: And I ***don't*** like yogurt.
Noni: Oh, I do. I think it's really nice. I have it occasionally with fruit and nuts.
Bev: But I love ice cream, of course, even though it's a dairy product.
Noni: Me _________. It's delicious!

Answers, page123.

Unit 10 - HAVING DINNER WITH FRIENDS - Part 6

FOCUS ON SPOKEN LANGUAGE

C) Uses of the word 'have'

The verb ***'have'*** is used in a variety of ways in English.
Look at these examples from Conversation 1 of this Unit.

I know what I'm going to ***have***...
I'm going to ***have*** a beer.
We're ***having*** an important meeting at work tomorrow.
It looks like I'll ***have*** to go and check it out myself.

As an ordinary verb, *'have'* can refer to a variety of different activities. For example:

- ***'have'*** can mean 'give birth to' eg. She's going to ***have*** a baby in March.
- ***'have'*** can mean 'engage in an activity'. eg. ***have*** a conversation; ***have*** a bath; ***have*** a party.
- ***'have'*** can mean 'undergo an experience'. eg. ***have*** an operation; ***have*** a good time.
- ***'have'*** can mean 'be part of a relationship'. eg. I ***have*** two brothers; I ***have*** a large family.
- ***'have'*** can mean 'possess a characteristic' eg I ***have*** black hair. They ***have*** poor eyesight.
- ***'have'*** can mean 'partake of food or drink'. eg. Let's ***have*** dinner; I'm going to ***have*** a beer.
- ***'have'*** can mean 'use/take' eg. '***Have*** a seat, please. The doctor will see you soon.'
- ***'have'*** can mean 'employ someone to do' eg. I ***have*** my windows cleaned every month.
- ***'have'*** can mean 'to own/ possess' eg. I ***have*** a driver's licence. I ***have*** a cat. I ***have*** a problem.

  In British English, ***'have got'*** is often used. eg. I***'ve got*** a problem. ***Have*** you ***got*** a new car?

  In other English speaking countries, notably America, ***do*** is used with ***have*** in questions and negatives. eg ***Do*** you ***have*** a problem? I ***don't have*** time. (Rather than 'I ***haven't got*** time.')

  Note: When the meaning is 'to own/ possess', there is no difference in meaning between,
  Do you ***have*** a car?/***Have*** you ***got*** a car?
  I ***have*** a car./I'***ve got*** a car.
  I ***don't have*** a car. /I ***haven't got*** a car.

Other uses of *'have'*:

- ***'have to'*** + verb expresses obligation (***have to*** has a similar meaning to ***must***) eg. I ***have to go*** to class now. (Also: I***'ve got to go*** to class now).
- ***have*** serves as an auxiliary (helper verb) in the present perfect tense.
  eg. I'***ve*** written a letter; ***Have*** you seen the movie, 'Star Wars?'; I ***have***n't finished .

LANGUAGE REVIEW THREE

(Units 7 - 10)

This section reviews some of the expressions which were introduced in Units 7, 8, 9 and 10 and gives you a chance to see what you have remembered.

Look at the pictures on the opposite page and decide what the people are saying by choosing from the expressions below.

Match each picture with an appropriate expression by writing the correct letter in the box next to each expression.

For extra practice, you could write the appropriate expression in the space provided in the picture.

1) 'Who polished off all the ice cream?' ☐

2) 'They're doing up the road and it's caused a lot of hold ups.' ☐

3) 'This looks like fun! Let's make the most of it.!' ☐

4) 'The traffic goes flat out along this road. It's very dangerous!' ☐

5) 'That ride was a bit hairy. I won't try that again!' ☐

6) 'My shout. I'll get this round.' ☐

7) 'No thankyou. It looks delicious but seafood doesn't agree with me'. ☐

8) 'You'll get sick if you keep burning the candle at both ends.' ☐

9) 'I'm going to put this behind me and get on with my life'. ☐

(Answers: page 123)

LANGUAGE REVIEW THREE - Units 7 - 10

ANSWERS TO UNIT ONE - A TELEPHONE ENQUIRY

Part 1

1) b) an Office Skills Course
2) a) last week
3) b) the class is full
4) a) next week
5) b) enrol in a computing course now

Part 5 Crossword

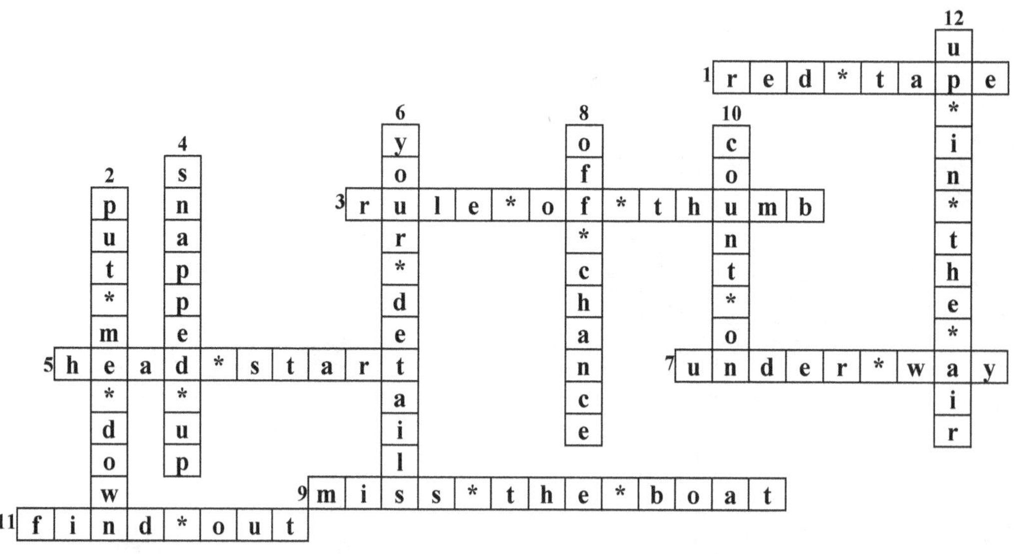

Part 6 Focus on Spoken Language

1) Would it still be possible to join this class?
2) Would it be possible to fax the enrolment form to me?
3) a) ✗ too polite/inappropriate
   b) ✓ appropriate
   c) ✓ appropriate
   d) ✗ too polite ('I'd like a coffee please.', is more appropriate.

ANSWERS TO UNIT TWO - TALKING ABOUT STUDY PROBLEMS

Part 1

1) c) her teacher is not pleased with her assignment;
   d) she may fail her course
2) b) leave / quit college
3) a) transfer to a different course.
   c) ask the teacher how she can improve her assignment

Part 5 Crossword

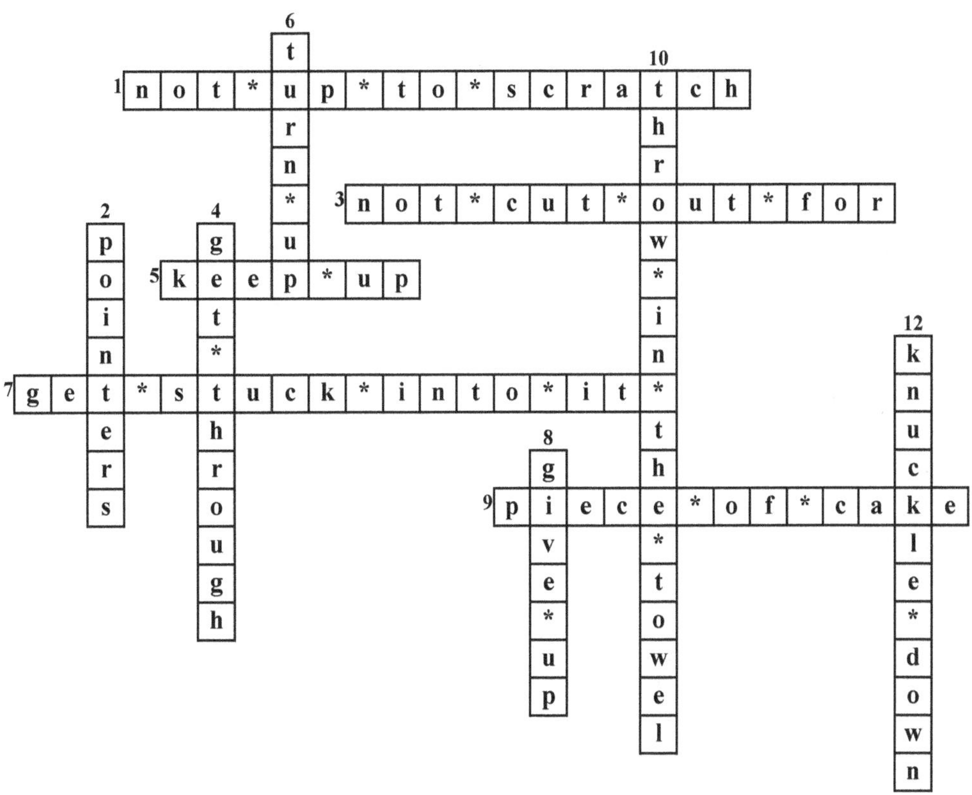

Part 6 Focus on Spoken Language

A) Making Suggestions

1) 'Well maybe you could transfer to a course more suited to you'.
2) 'Well in that case, why don't you go and talk to your teacher'?

Most direct	1	Go and talk to your teacher.
	2	You should go and talk to your teacher.
	3	Why don't you go and talk to your teacher?
Least direct	4	Well, maybe you could go and talk to your teacher.

B) Giving Reasons

No. I've got Buckley's chance of getting into another course now – it's too late. ***Besides***, I'd prefer to see this course through if I'm going to do anything.

C) Pronunciation and Spelling

Words with a short vowel sound /ɪ/	Words with a long vowel sound /i:/
beginning, *giving*, *thinking*, *this*, *didn't*, *things*, *think*, *in*	*piece*, *received*, *seems*, *teacher*

Practice

/ɪ/ **short** vowel sound (eg. s**i**t)	/i:/ **long** vowel sound (eg. s**ea**t)
English, *busy*, *pretty*, *bill*, *big*, *mystery*	*seize*, *tea*, *key*, *magazine*, *feet*

ANSWERS TO UNIT THREE - TALKING ABOUT EMPLOYMENT

Part 1

skills and talents (things you can do)	***abilities***
summary of education and work experience	***résumé (also CV)***
emergency medical treatment	***first aid***
training and educational accomplishments	***qualifications***
the work of keeping things in good condition	***maintenance***
manager	***supervisor***
lawfully set guidelines of payment	***award wage***
related to the subject receiving attention	***relevant***

1) b) a maintenance worker
   c) an office worker
2) a) a current driver's licence
   b) first aid certificate
3) a) improve his resume
   c) write a letter of application

Part 5 Crossword

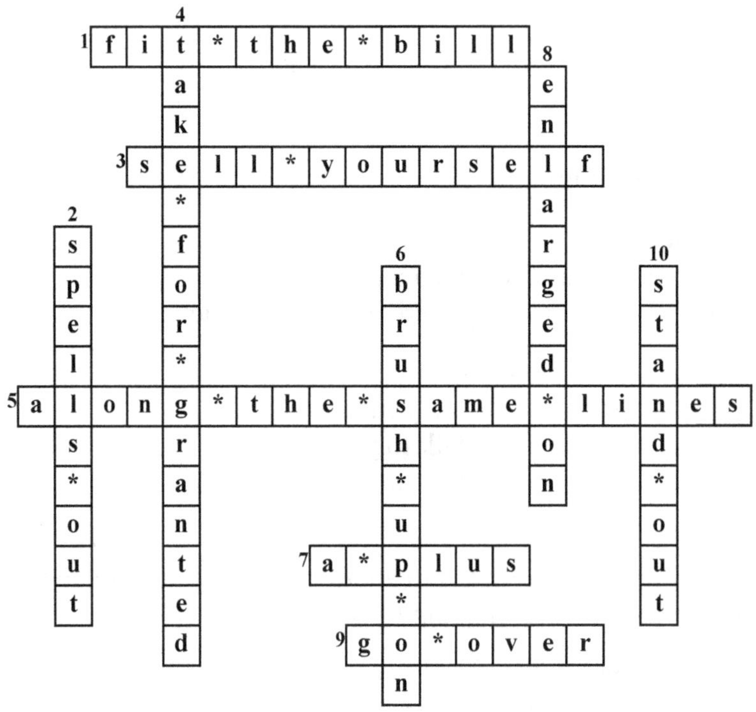

Part 6 Focus on Spoken Language

**C) Talking about the Past (using present perfect and simple past tenses)
Practice Answers**

Some possible verbs are:-

Have you ***completed*** your training yet?	Yes, I ***finished*** my course in 1997
Have you ***used*** this computer program before?	No, I ***used*** another program in my last job.
Have you ***worked*** in a shoe factory before?	Yes, I ***worked*** in a big shoe factory in Taiwan.
Have you ***operated*** this type of machine before?	Yes, I ***operated*** one like this in my last job.

ANSWERS TO LANGUAGE REVIEW ONE - UNITS 1 - 3

1) E **2) F** **3) B**

4) H **5) G** **6) I**

7) C **8) D** **9) A**

ANSWERS TO UNIT FOUR - TECHNOLOGY AND BUSINESS

Part 1

a person controlled by someone/something - ***slave***	change to a new system - ***changeover***
a branch of production/manufacture - ***industry***	expensive/ costing a lot of money - ***costly***

1) b) business is not going well
2) b) the printing industry
3) a) invest in some better technology
4) b) thinks we are becoming slaves to technology

Part 5 Crossword

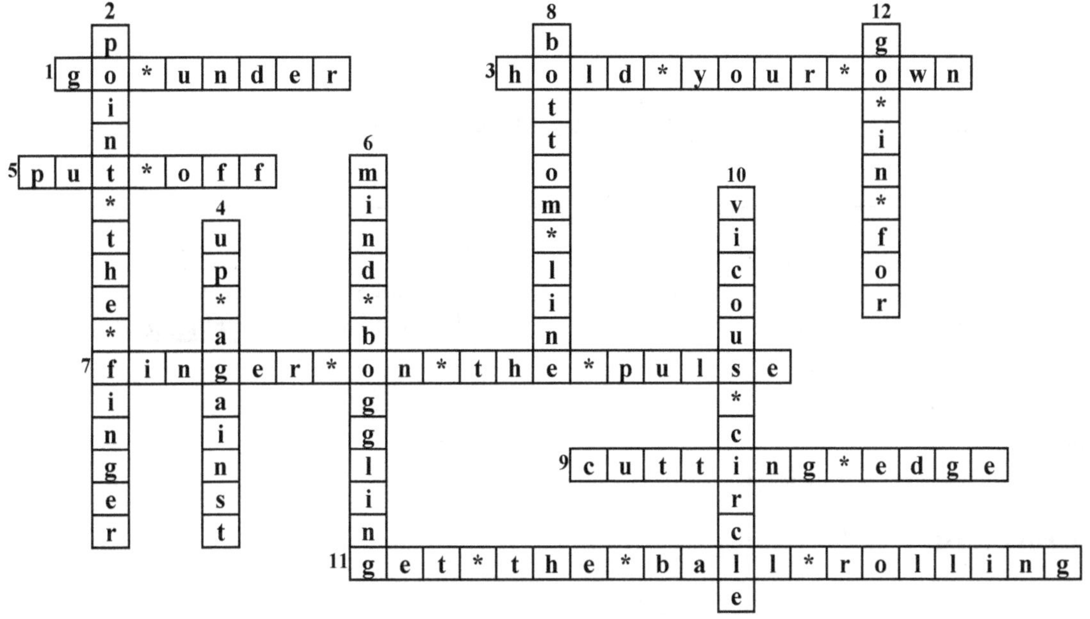

Part 6 Focus on Spoken Language

A) Listening Practice

words with one syllable	words with two syllables	words with three syllables	words with four syllables
know	mi/nute	a/ny/thing	tech/no/lo/gy
sales	dis/cuss	su/gges/ted	
months	fa/lling	in/dus/try	
good	be/tween		
	be/fore		
	fin/ger		
	a/long		
	be/tter		

ANSWERS TO UNIT FOUR - TECHNOLOGY AND BUSINESS

B) Dictionary Practice

***min**ute* - *the **first** syllable is stressed.*
be***tween*** - *the **second** syllable is stressed*
be***fore*** - *the **second** syllable is stressed*
***fin**ger* - *the **first** syllable is stressed*
along - *the **second** syllable is stressed*

C) Discourse Markers

Assistant: So when do you think we'll start the changeover?
Manager: The sooner the better, ***I suppose***. There're some big changes to make and I'm not really looking forward to them. You know .... ***I wonder*** whether all this new technology is really making our lives easier. ***It seems*** that we've created a vicious circle......
Assistant: What do you mean?
Manager: Well, technology's supposed to have given us more time and freedom but ***it seems*** we're becoming slaves to technology.....

D) 'I'd prefer it as hot as possible.' means 'the ***hotter*** the better'
'I'd prefer it as light as possible.' means 'the ***lighter*** the better'
'I'd prefer it as small as possible.' means 'the ***smaller*** the better'
'I'd prefer it as clear as possible.' means 'the ***clearer*** the better'

ANSWERS TO UNIT FIVE - POLITICS AND GOVERNMENT

Part 1

period of time in government - ***term***
first choice, importance - ***priority***
government by the people - ***democracy***
a political group - ***party***
important subject - ***issue***
judge, find faults - ***criticise***

1) b) who to vote for
2) b) education
3) b) Ali should become a politician

Part 5 Crossword

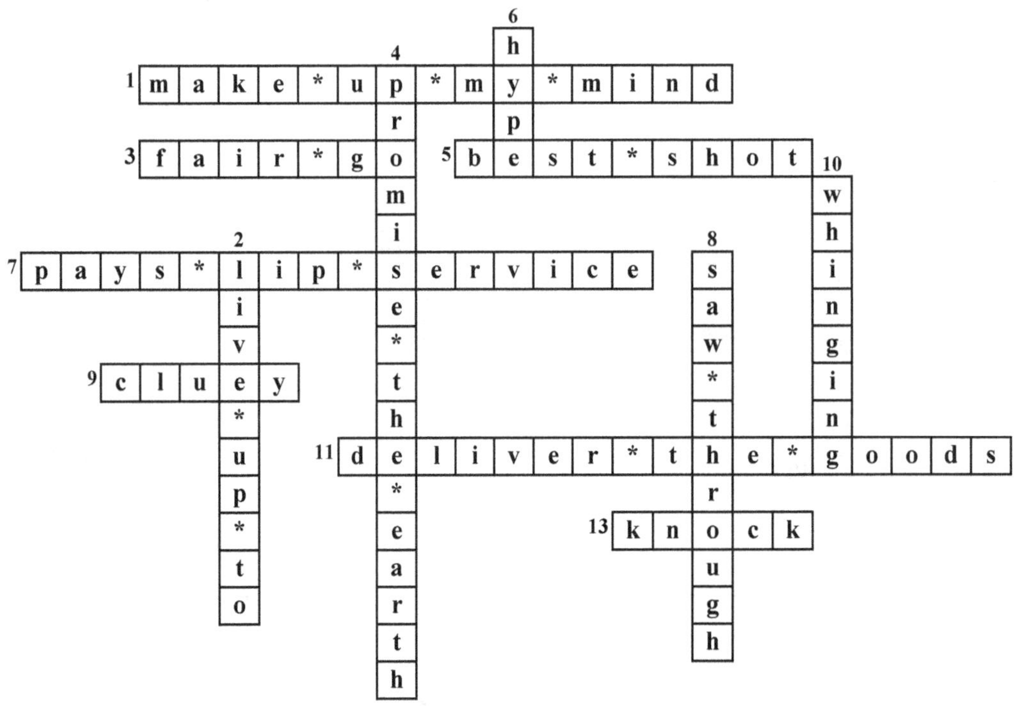

ANSWERS TO UNIT FIVE - POLITICS AND GOVERNMENT

Part 6 Focus on Spoken Language - Conversation Strategies

A) Agreeing and Disagreeing politely

Expressions showing agreement	*Expressions showing disagreement*
That's for sure. ***You're right there.***	***you've got a point but......*** ***Yeah, but don't you think....*** ***I can't agree with you there...*** ***No way!***

B) Using Pronouns

1) ***They*** refers to ***the company/employers.***

2) ***They*** refers to ***scientists/people who lived in the past.***

3) ***They*** refers to ***the management of the supermarket.***

C) Pronouns - pronunciation and spelling

PRACTICE

1) ***We're*** very upset because we lost our camera when we ***were*** overseas last month.

2) ***He's*** very happy that he's passed ***his*** driving test!

3) ***You're*** much taller than ***your*** sister but she's older than you, isn't she?

4) The cat has eaten ***its*** dinner and now ***it's*** sitting on the window sill.

5) ***They're*** coming by train because ***their*** car is being repaired.

ANSWERS TO UNIT SIX - A NEW VENTURE - MAKING DECISIONS

Part 1

benefits, good points - ***advantages***	making definite decisions - ***decisive***
negative points - ***disadvantages***	things that are possible - ***possibilities***

1) b) a coffee shop.

2) b) High Street

3) a) special introductory prices; b) an 'Under New Management' sign.

4) c) write a list of the pros and cons.

Part 5 Crossword

Part 6 Focus on Spoken Language

A) 2) '***one***' refers to ***coffee shop***
3) '***it***' refers to ***coffee shop***; '***one***' also refers to ***coffee shop.***
4) '***It***" refers to ***coffee shop***

PRACTICE

I want to buy a new dress for the party but I'm having trouble finding the right ***one.*** I've seen some lovely ***ones*** but I'd like to get ***one*** with long sleeves.

B) Giving Advice

If I were you, ***I'd write a list of the pros and cons of starting a business from scratch*** or buying one that's already established and weigh up the possibilities on both sides before making any decisions.

C) Weighing up the pros and cons -Talking about Future Possibilities

It'd save me a lot of time, money and hard work.

D) Revision

words with one syllable	words with two syllables	words with three syllables	words with four syllables
know **through** **sale** **plunge**	**to/ying** **co/ffee** **a/bout** **bus/(i)ness** **('i' not pronounced)**	**i/de/a** **re/mem/ber** **news/pa/per**	**se/ri/ous/ly**

ANSWERS TO UNIT SIX - A NEW VENTURE - MAKING DECISIONS

Syllable Stress

Now decide which syllable is ***stressed*** in each of the following words.

idea - the ***second (middle)*** syllable is stressed.
about - the ***second*** syllable is stressed.
re**mem**ber - the ***second (middle)*** syllable is stressed.
seriously - the ***first*** syllable is stressed.
business - the ***first*** syllable is stressed

ANSWERS TO LANGUAGE REVIEW TWO - UNITS 4 - 6

1) E	**4) I**	**7) C**
2) F	**5) D**	**8) B**
3) H	**6) G**	**9) A**

ANSWERS TO UNIT SEVEN - TALKING ABOUT THE PAST

Part 1

playful but unacceptable conduct - ***mischief***	unhappy/angry because of problems - ***bitter***
a sudden, bad experience - ***a shock***	improve/return to a good situation - ***recover***
being able to support yourself - ***independent***	things that happen to us during life -***experiences***

1) a) party all weekend.
2) a) his parents had been killed in an accident.
3) a) he had learnt a lot from his experiences.

Part 5 Crossword

										6 m				8 g														
1 b	2 u	r	n	*	4 t	h	e	*	c	a	n	d	l	e	*	a	t	*	b	o	t	h	*	e	n	d	12 s	
	p				a					k				t													i	
	s				k					e				*													c	
	*		3 k	e	e	p	*	i	t	*	u	p		o			10 g										k	
	a				s					t				n			e										i	
	n				*					h				*			t										e	
	d				m					e				w			*											
	*				e					*				5 i	n	*	o	n	e	*	p	i	e	c	e			
	d				*					m				t			v											
	o				b					o				h			e											
	w				a					s							r											
	n				c				7 s	t	a	n	d	*	o	n	*	m	y	*	o	w	n	*	f	e	e	t
	s				k					*																		
								9 a	r	o	u	n	d	*	t	h	e	*	c	o	r	n	e	r				
										f																		

Part 6 Focus on Spoken English

1) We used to get up to some mischief.
   We used to burn the candle at both ends most weekends.
2) We'd party all night and then go straight to work the next day without any sleep.....or we'd take a sickie and go to the beach.
3) No, Dan doesn't do those things now.

ANSWERS TO UNIT SEVEN - TALKING ABOUT THE PAST

Part 6 B) Pronunciation - Practice 1

words ending in /d/	words ending with /t/
happened killed received	talked

Practice 2

ed pronounced as /d/	*ed* pronounced as /t/	*ed* pronounced as /əd/
loved arrived	looked worked washed	waited included started

C) Pronunciation /ɪ/ and /e/

/ɪ/	/e/
b*u*sy pr*e*tty b*i*ll b*i*g m*y*stery *E*nglish	h*ea*d s*ai*d *e*gg

ANSWERS TO UNIT EIGHT - ASKING FOR DIRECTIONS

Part 1

choice - **option**
go around/stay away from - **avoid**
bridge over a road/railway - **overpass**
smaller/less important streets - **backstreets**
a curve in the road - **bend**
business time (for traffic) - **peak hour**

1) b) Fairgrove
2) b) he travelled through the area ten years ago
3) a) the old road. b) through the backstreets
4) b) through the backstreets

Part 5 Crossword

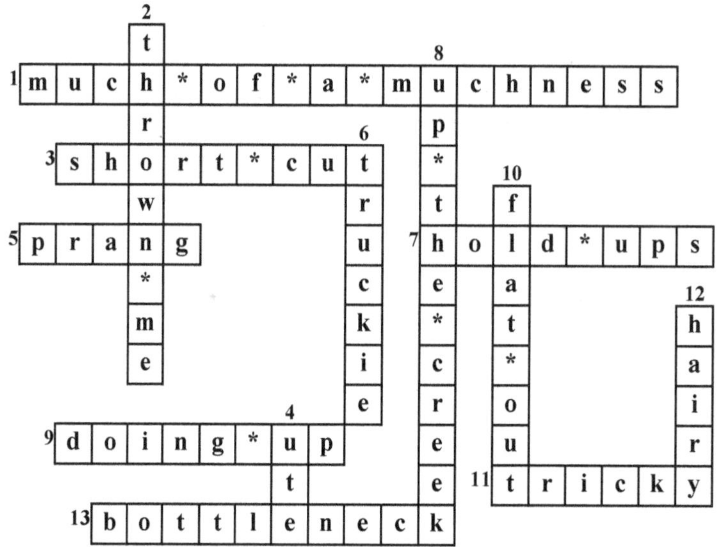

ANSWERS TO UNIT EIGHT - ASKING FOR DIRECTIONS

Part 6 Focus on Spoken English

A) *Giving Instructions*

IMPERATIVE	*SITUATION*
Mix the sugar and milk together.	instruction for a recipe
'***Sit*** down and be quiet.'	instruction from parent to small child
Go up the stairs and then turn right.	direction
'***Be*** careful!'	warning regarding danger
'***Leave*** the building now!'	command to show authority
Deal five cards to each player.	instruction for a game

B) *Pronunciation and Spelling*

'give' is different (pronounced as /gɪv/)

C) *Words beginning with the letter 'u'*

1) ***U- ie*** (pronounced **/ju:i:/**), and ***ute*** (pronounced **/ju:t/**)
2) The word ***umbrella*** begins with a short vowel sound /ʌ/, so is different .
   All the other words begin with a long sound, **/ju:/**

ANSWERS TO UNIT NINE - FUTURE PLANS AND POSSIBILITIES

Part 1

a target for the future- ***goal***
idea, belief, opinion - ***philosophy***
happily, with desire - ***eagerly***
determined to succeed - ***ambitious***
unpaid work - ***voluntary (work)***
a useful situation -***opportunity***

1) b) visit her family;
   c) look for a job
2) a) do some voluntary work
3) a) people have to plan if they want to succeed.
4) a) ambitious.

Part 5 Crossword

ANSWERS TO UNIT NINE - FUTURE PLANS AND POSSIBILITIES

Part 6 Focus on Spoken Language

A) ***PRACTICE 1*** Kerri: I suppose, I ***'ll*** just ***play*** it by ear.
Kerri: I guess, I ***'ll look*** for a job too.
Chris: I'***ll*** just ***get*** my bag.

PRACTICE 2
1st Speaker: This box is very heavy! 2nd Speaker: Wait a minute. I***'ll help*** you.
1st Speaker: Oh, I forgot to post this letter! 2nd Speaker: Don't worry. I'***ll post*** it later.

B)

Yes, I'***m***	***going to***	***visit*** my family in the country for a week.
…… I'***m***	***going to***	***look*** for a job…….as a tour guide if possible.
That's what I'***m***	***going to***	***do*** if I don't get a job straight away.
Look, I'***m***	***going to***	***get*** a cup of coffee. Would you like one?

PRACTICE
Sue: 'What are you going to do on Saturday?'
Pat: 'I'm not sure yet. I think I ***will*** stay home and finish my homework.'
Sue: 'Jenni and I are ***going to*** go to the beach. Would you like to come?'
Pat: 'Yes. That sounds great! I ***will*** finish my homework on Sunday instead.'
Sue: 'OK. We're ***going to*** catch the bus at 8 a.m.'
Pat: 'OK I ***will*** meet you at the bus stop then. What are you ***going to*** take for lunch?'
Sue: 'I'm not sure yet. I guess I ***will*** just take some fruit and a sandwich.'

C) Kerri……I can see ***you're going to*** go places.

PRACTICE: Various sentences are possible.
eg. The batter will hit the ball./ The wicket keeper will catch the ball

REVISION & PRACTICE - Talking about the Future

Rai: What ***are*** you ***going to do*** while you're on holidays next week?
Jan: I ***am going to stay*** (or ***am staying***) with my sister, Kate, and help her look after her two small sons.
Rai: Why? Is she sick?
Jan: No. She ***is having*** (or ***is going to have***) another baby.
Rai: Really? In that case, I ***will call*** her on the phone tonight and congratulate her.
Jan: Oh good! I'm sure, she ***will be*** happy to hear from you.
Rai: In fact, I think I ***will go*** to the shops tomorrow and buy a present for her. Any ideas?
Jan: Well, the weather ***is going to be*** (or ***will be***) hot when the baby's born…
Rai: I know! I ***will buy*** her a fan!

ANSWERS TO UNIT TEN - HAVING DINNER WITH FRIENDS

Part 1

a) a place where customers collect their meal on a tray from a counter - ***cafeteria***
a meal in which customers select from a variety of displayed food - ***buffet***
a restaurant where a variety of meals may be ordered from a menu - ***a la carte***

b) an 'a la carte' meal.

1) b) one
2) b) wine
3) b) one friend said it was OK but the other friend thought it was very funny.

ANSWERS TO UNIT TEN - HAVING DINNER WITH FRIENDS

Part 5 Crossword

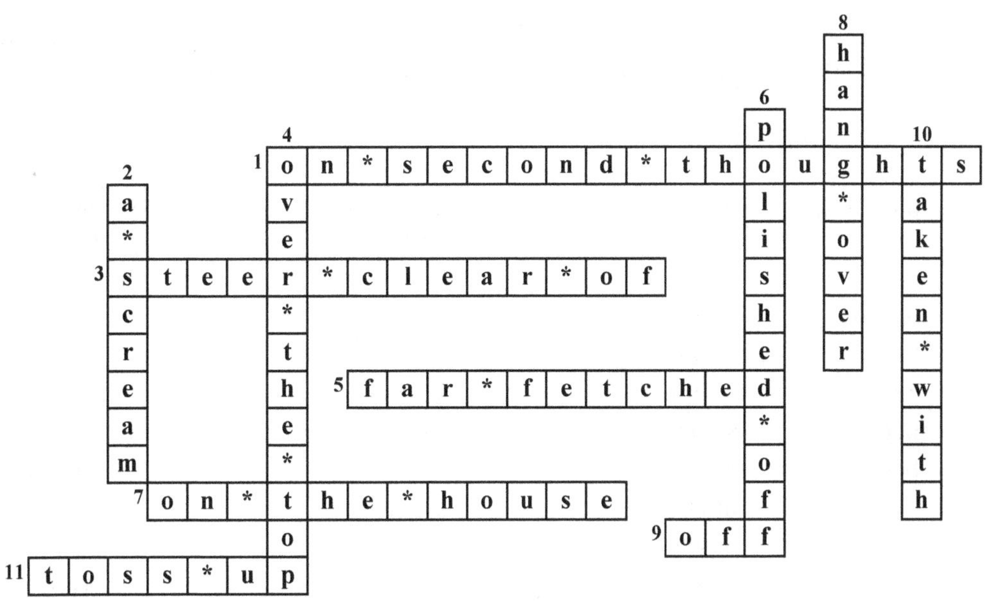

Part 6 Focus on Spoken Language

A) Pronunciation and Spelling (different sounds of the letter 'o')

words with /ɒ/ (short vowel sound)	words with /ɔː/ (long vowel sound)	words with /əʊ/ (diphthong sound)
toss	*pork*	*roast* *don't*
chops	*prawns*	*won't* *go*
on	*sauce*	*no* *roast*
off	*North*	*told*

B) 1)

Lee: Mm…I love prawns too but spicy food doesn't agree with me. So I ***won't*** have that.
Julie: ***Me neither***. I'm going to steer clear of prawns from now on. I had some that were off a few months ago and I can't stand them now.

2)

Lee: Now what'll I have…..I think, I'***ll*** go for the roast.
Julie: ***Me too***. The roast beef is always good here.

3)
Bev: I ***don't*** eat dairy products these days. They don't agree with me.
Noni: Me ***neither***. I'm allergic to milk.
Bev: I ***can't*** stand cheese.
Noni: Me ***neither***. It makes me feel sick.
Bev: And I ***don't*** like yogurt.
Noni: Oh, I do. I think it's really nice. I have it occasionally with fruit and nuts.
Bev: But I love ice cream, of course, even though it's a dairy product.
Noni: Me ***too***. It's delicious!

ANSWERS TO LANGUAGE REVIEW THREE

1) G **4) C** **7) H**
2) D **5) E** **8) B**
3) A **6) F** **9) I**

Information about English verbs

A verb may consist of one or more words. Auxiliary verbs help the base verb to form tenses, questions and other expressions. The principal auxiliary verbs are ***be/is/am/are***, ***have/has*** and ***do***.

The letters ***ed*** are added to most verbs to form a past participle or past simple tense. eg. work→work***ed***. However, for some verbs, the spelling is ***irregular*** (doesn't follow the usual rules). eg. see→saw→seen.

A List of some Irregular Verbs:

base verb **infinitive** **present simple**	**past simple**	**past participle** for the present perfect tense use with *have/has*
be/am/is/are	was/were	been
beat	beat	beaten
become	became	become
begin	began	begun
bend	bent	bent
bite	bit	bitten
blow	blew	blown
break	broke	broken
bring	brought	brought
build	built	built
burn	burnt/burned	burnt/burned
buy	bought	bought
catch	caught	caught
choose	chose	chosen
come	came	come
dig	dug	dug
do	did	done
draw	drew	drawn
drink	drank	drunk
drive	drove	driven
eat	ate	eaten
fall	fell	fallen
feed	fed	fed
feel	felt	felt
fight	fought	fought
find	found	found
fly	flew	flown
forget	forgot	forgotten
forgive	forgave	forgiven
get	got	got
give	gave	given
go	went	gone
grow	grew	grown
have	had	had
hear	heard	heard
hide	hid	hidden
hold	held	held
keep	kept	kept
know	knew	known
lay	laid	laid
lead	led	led
leave	left	left

base verb **infinitive** **present simple**	**past simple**	**past participle** for the present perfect tense use with *have/has*
lend	lent	lent
light	lit	lit
lose	lost	lost
make	made	made
mean	meant	meant
meet	met	met
pay	paid	paid
read /ri:d/	read /red/	read /red/
ride	rode	ridden
ring	rang	rung
rise	rose	risen
run	ran	run
say	said	said
see	saw	seen
sell	sold	sold
send	sent	sent
show	showed	shown
sing	sang	sung
sink	sank	sunk
sit	sat	sat
sleep	slept	slept
speak	spoke	spoken
spell	spelt	spelt
spend	spent	spent
spring	sprang	sprung
stand	stood	stood
steal	stole	stolen
sting	stung	stung
swear	swore	sworn
swim	swam	swum
swing	swung	swung
take	took	taken
teach	taught	taught
tear /teə/	tore	torn
tell	told	told
think	thought	thought
throw	threw	thrown
understand	understood	understood
wake	woke	woken
wear	wore	worn
win	won	won
write	wrote	written

UNDERSTANDING EVERYDAY AUSTRALIAN

There are many Australian colloquial words which end in 'ie' and 'y'.
Not all Australians *use* these expressions but they would be familiar with their meaning.
Here are some examples for your reference.

EVERYDAY EXPRESSION	DEFINITION
Aussie............................	Australian
barbie............................	barbecue
bickie............................	biscuit
billy..............................	container for boiling water (boil the billy = make tea/coffee)
blowie............................	blowfly
brekkie..........................	breakfast
brickie..........................	bricklayer
bushie..........................	a person who lives in the country/bush
chippie..........................	a carpenter/someone who works with wood
Chrissie........................	Christmas
cocky............................	cockatoo - a type of native parrot (also a farmer)
cossie..........................	swimming costume (also called *togs* or *bathers*)
deli.............................	delicatessen/a shop selling cold meat & cheeses
lolly............................	a sweet/candy
mozzies........................	mosquitoes
nightie..........................	a woman's night-dress (to wear in bed)
pollies..........................	politicians
possie..........................	position/place
postie..........................	post man/woman
pressie........................	present/gift
rellie...........................	family relative (in-laws)
sickie..........................	a day off work (with the excuse of being sick)
stubbie........................	a small bottle of beer
telly............................	television
truckie........................	truck driver
u-ie............................	U-turn (to turn around and drive the opposite way)
undies........................	under clothes/underwear
vegies........................	vegetables

Unit 1 - A TELEPHONE ENQUIRY – REFERENCE LIST

EVERYDAY EXPRESSIONS	DEFINITIONS
hold the line…………………………………..	wait a moment
put (you) through…………………………..	connect you to the department/person
under way…………………………………..	in progress
put (you) down …………………………..	write your name on the list
found out………………………………………	learnt/discovered/heard about
a rule of thumb…………………………..	a rule for general guidance
take (your) details………………………..	record your name, address etc
the off chance……………………………..	the slight possibility
pull out……………………………………..	withdraw/cancel
from time to time………………………..	sometimes
red tape……………………………………..	official rules/procedures
up in the air………………………………	undecided
I wouldn't count on it……………………	don't expect it to happen/rely on it
a goer………………………………………	a useful/successful project
a head start……………………………………	an advantage
I may as well……………………………….	I should (it's probably a good opportunity).
ASAP………………………………………..	as soon as possible
snapped up………………………………..	taken/accepted quickly
miss the boat……………………………..	miss/lose an opportunity
this arvo………………………………………..	this afternoon

Unit 2 - TALKING ABOUT STUDY PROBLEMS – REFERENCE LIST

EVERYDAY EXPRESSIONS	DEFINITIONS
What's up?......................................	What's the problem?
not keeping up..................................	not progressing at the expected rate
too laid-back..................................	too relaxed/lazy
a piece of cake..................................	an easy task
turn up to..	attend
a rude awakening..............................	an unpleasant surprise
not up to scratch...............................	not good enough/not of an acceptable standard/level
drop out	quit/stop participating
not cut out for..................................	not suited to
throw in the towel.............................	stop trying/participating
put in	(time/work) invested
giving up...	stopping effort
Buckley's chance...............................	little or no chance of (success)
see (something) through.....................	persist/continue (to completion)
knuckle down....................................	work hard
some pointers....................................	some advice
get stuck into it................................	try/work hard
catch up...	reach/achieve the required level (after being behind)
get through......................................	pass/complete
give it a go.......................................	try
That's more like it!	That's a better idea!

Unit 3 - TALKING ABOUT EMPLOYMENT – REFERENCE LIST

EVERYDAY EXPRESSIONS	DEFINITIONS
looked over (something)	examined
go over (something)...........................	review/discuss
enlarge on (something)........................	explain in more detail
take for granted................................	assume/suppose (something) will be known
spell out..	explain clearly
stand out..	be noticeable
sell yourself....................................	promote your value
something along the same lines............	similar to
keep going......................................	continue
it just so happens..............................	by chance
take it..	suppose
come in handy..................................	be useful
a plus...	an advantage
fit the bill.......................................	be exactly the right person (or thing) for the job
bring up to date.................................	change to include the most recent information/ ideas
put together.....................................	compose/make
be looking at....................................	expect (a certain amount)
and so on..	and other things
a rough idea.....................................	an estimation
(to) set up.......................................	arrange/organise
brush up on.....................................	revise/review/practise
rusty..	weak/impaired due to lack of practice (needing of practice)

Unit 4 -TECHNOLOGY AND BUSINESS – REFERENCE LIST

EVERYDAY EXPRESSIONS	DEFINITIONS
falling off………………………………...	decreasing
between you and me ………………………...	confidentially (this information is private)
pointing the finger………………………	saying the problem was caused by (you)
go in for…………………………………...	get/seek/show interest in (something)
hold our own……………………………...	keep/defend our position
go along with……………………………	agree with
bite the bullet……………………………..	make an important/difficult decision
up against ………………………………	competing with
folding…………………………………….	failing/closing (business)
jump on the bandwagon…………………..	follow the popular course
go under…………………………………...	fail (in business)
be at the cutting edge……………………	be involved with the most advanced/recent developments
keep your finger on the pulse……………	know the latest information
putting off…………………………………	delaying/postponing
the bottom line……………………………	the basic truth
the sooner the better……………………..	as soon as possible
a vicious circle…………………………...	a cycle (of problems) in which the solution to one problem creates more problems
mind-boggling……………………………...	unbelievable/amazing/difficult to understand
get my head around………………………	understand/accept
go with the flow…………………………...	accept changes (in life)
get the ball rolling………………………..	start the project/activity

Unit 5 - POLITICS AND GOVERNMENT – REFERENCE LIST

EVERYDAY EXPRESSIONS	DEFINITIONS
make up my mind...................................	decide
promise the earth	promise great things
the run-up to...	period of time before (an event)
live up to (a promise).............................	honour/fulfil (a promise)
pay lip service to (something)....................	talk about an issue without sincerity (without meaning what is said)
haven't got much to show	have not produced results
(term) is up	(term/period of time) is finished
a fair go	fair treatment
deliver the goods	produce the promised results
six of one and half a dozen of the other...	there will be no difference in the final result
knock	criticise
pollies..	politicians
give it their best shot................................	try to achieve the best result
face the music..	accept responsibility and criticism (for an action or decision)
weigh up..	consider carefully (the available options)
see through	not be deceived by (someone or something)
hype	publicity
whinging	complaining
sit up and take notice................................	become interested
cluey..	clever/knowledgeable
No way!..	I'd never do that!

Unit 6 - A NEW VENTURE – MAKING DECISIONS – REFERENCE LIST

EVERYDAY EXPRESSIONS	DEFINITIONS
toying with the idea...........................	thinking about
come across......................................	find by chance
going for a song................................	being sold very cheaply
take the plunge.................................	take a decisive step
from scratch......................................	from the beginning without help
up and running..................................	operating
on the grapevine................................	(information) heard through other people
going downhill..................................	needing repair/ not cared for
get rid of...	dispose of (it)
run-down...	neglected/ in a bad condition
elbow grease......................................	hard work/physical effort
up my sleeve......................................	in my mind
off the ground....................................	into successful operation
put (you) off......................................	discourage (you)
get your fingers burnt.........................	suffer a bad experience
pros and cons.....................................	advantages and disadvantages
weigh up	consider
take into account...............................	consider
look into (it)......................................	investigate
drawbacks...	disadvantages
do (my) homework............................	research/investigate
go ahead...	continue/proceed

Unit 7 - TALKING ABOUT THE PAST – REFERENCE LIST

EVERYDAY EXPRESSIONS	DEFINITIONS
takes me back	makes me remember
to get up to (something)	do/be engaged in (an activity)
in one piece	alive and unharmed
crazy	foolish (but exciting)
burn the candle at both ends	have very little sleep (due to too much activity)
take a sickie	have a day off work (with the excuse of being sick)
keep (that) up	continue with (that activity)
turned upside down	completely changed (usually in a negative way)
get over (it)	recover
I'd rather not go into it	I'd rather not talk about/discuss it.
Fair enough	I understand. I accept what you say.
strike me as (something)	seem/appear to me as (something)
put this behind me	recover from (this unhappy experience)
get on with (something)	proceed/continue with (something)
haven't looked back	have progressed/succeeded
take the rough with the smooth	accept both good and bad experiences in life
can't turn the clock back	can't go back to the past
ups and downs	good and bad experience in life
stand on my own feet	be independent
around the corner	in the future
make the most of	fully use and enjoy

Unit 8 - ASKING FOR DIRECTIONS – REFERENCE LIST

EVERYDAY EXPRESSIONS	DEFINITIONS
Are you right there?...........................	Do you need some help? (Can I help you?)
after	seeking/looking for
a bottleneck...	a crowded section of road
bumper to bumper traffic.........................	very slow moving traffic
K's...	kilometres
doing up..	repairing/improving
hold ups...	delays
thrown me...	confused me
tricky...	difficult/confusing
CBD...	central business district
hairy..	frightening/dangerous
truckies..	truck drivers
go flat out.....................................	go very quickly
a short cut..	a shorter way
do a U-ie...	do a U-turn (turn around and drive the opposite way)
ute..	utility truck
a dogleg...	a bend in the road (shaped like a dog's back leg).
follow your nose.......................................	go straight ahead/go the obvious way
much of a muchness..................................	almost the same result
a prang...	a car accident
be up the creek...	in trouble/difficulty
No worries!..	You are welcome.

Unit 9 - FUTURE PLANS AND POSSIBILITIES – REFERENCE LIST

EVERYDAY EXPRESSIONS	DEFINITIONS
just about	almost
play it by ear	wait and see what happens
looking forward to	eagerly awaiting
half hearted (about)	disinterested (only half interested)
let's face it	we must be realistic
every Tom, Dick and Harry	a lot of (ordinary) people
straight away	immediately
twiddling my thumbs	doing nothing
wrapped in the idea	happy about the idea
killing two birds with one stone	achieving two things/results with one action
paving the way	preparing the way
you never know	there is a possibility
down the track	in the future
have to hand it to (you)	have to admire/congratulate (you)
have it all worked out	have everything planned and organised
turn up	arrive/occur/happen
out of the blue	unexpectedly (without planning)
set (our) sights on	decide and aim for
go for it!	strive/try hard (to get what we want)
go places	be successful
get my act together	get organised

Unit 10 - HAVING DINNER WITH FRIENDS – REFERENCE LIST

EVERYDAY EXPRESSIONS	DEFINITIONS
a toss up..	a choice/decision
doesn't agree with me........................	isn't good for my health
steer clear of....................................	avoid
off..	bad/stale
can't stand..	dislike very much
on the house......................................	at no cost (at the management's expense)
I don't blame you..............................	I understand your decision.
go for..	choose/have
my shout..	it's my treat/I will pay for you.
round..	set of drinks (one for each member)
I'm easy...	I'll be happy with either choice/ I don't mind.
on second thoughts...........................	after thinking more about (it)
a hangover..	a headache etc. caused by too much alcohol
polish off...	finish
a scream...	a very funny (thing)
a send up..	an entertaining mimic (joke)
taken with...	impressed with/by (something)
over the top	exaggerated/extreme
far-fetched..	unbelievable
check it out.......................................	see/investigate

Phonemic Chart of English Sounds

Below each sound symbol are examples of words containing the sound.

Vowel sounds

æ (short sound) black	e (short sound) red	ɒ (short sound) .... dots	ə (unstressed sound) other brother
ɑː (long sound) car	ʊ (short sound) good	ʌ (short sound) fun	ɪ (short sound) pink
ɜː (long sound) purple	uː (long sound) blue	ɔː (long sound) four more	iː (long sound) green

Diphthong (two vowel) sounds

eɪ grey	ɔɪ boy	əʊ (also oʊ) yellow gold	ɪə clear beer
eə (also ɛə) hair	aɪ bright lime	ʊə tour	aʊ brown mouse

Consonant sounds

p pet pig	b big bag	t tell two	d dirty dog
tʃ Chinese child	dʒ just joking	k keep cool	g good girl
f fill four	v very vivid	θ think thin	ð other brother
s sad song	z zig-zag	ʃ short sheep	ʒ measure Asia
m milk man	n no never	ŋ long song	h hot hill
l little line	r rice	w wet winter	j yes you

As the pronunciation of some English vowel sounds varies across and within countries, the examples given on this chart are intended as a general guide

NOTES

Use this page to record everyday expressions that you hear during your daily activities.

Boyer Educational Resources books and audio CDs

'Understanding Everyday Australian' – series (books with audio CD)

Readers (A5), Audio CDs, Language workbooks

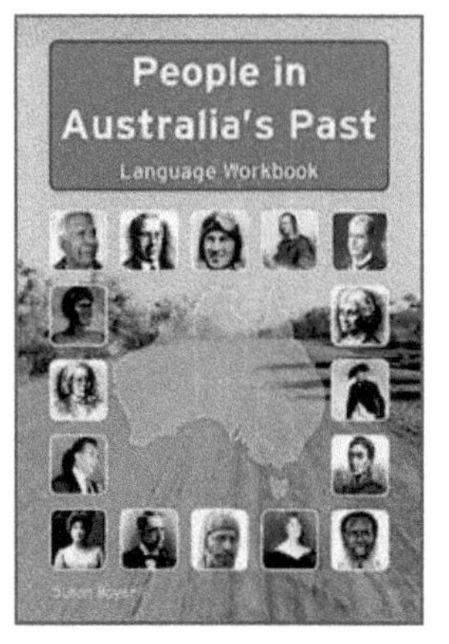

'Understanding Spoken English' – (books with audio CD) international editions

Spelling and Pronunciation for English Language Learners

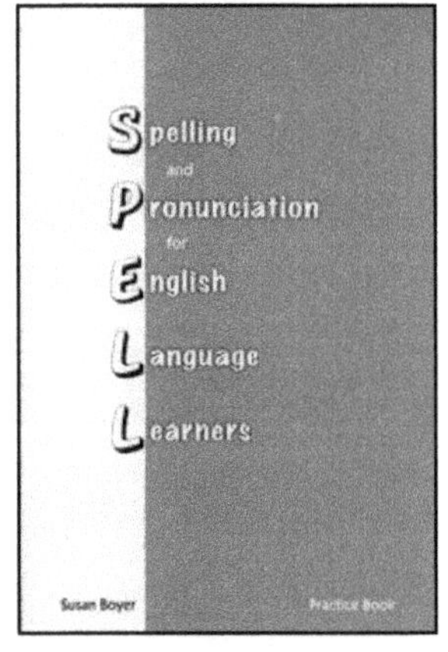

Understanding English Pronunciation

Word Building Activities for beginners of English

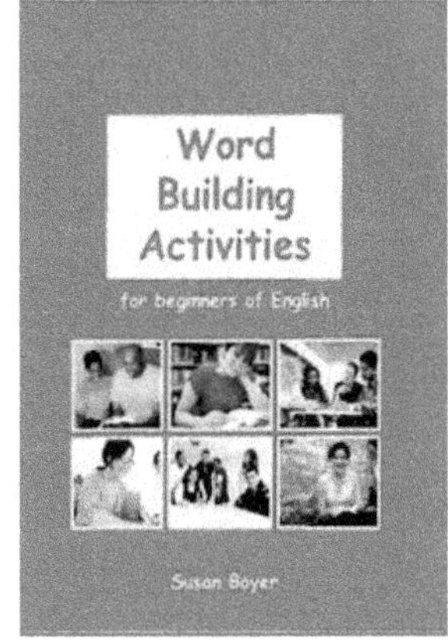

English Language Skills Level One

English Language Skills
Level 1
Student's Workbook

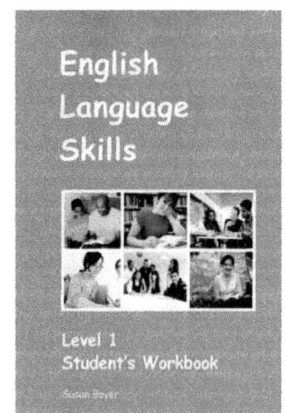

Spiral bound Teacher's Books with photocopiable activities such as surveys, role-cards & matching activities:

All our teacher's books are A4 size. Student's books contain language exercises and answers.

Boyer Educational Resources

Office phone/fax: +61 (0)2 4739 1538 **e-mail: boyer@eftel.net.au**
websites: www.boyereducation.com.au **www.englishebooks.com**

	Title	ISBN	RRP
Focus on Australian content	People in Australia's past - their stories, their achievements - A5 Reader	978 1 877074 34 9	$12.95
	People in Australia's past - audio CD	978 1 877074 35 6	$19.95
	People in Australia's past - language workbook A4 (156 pages)	978 1 877074 36 3	$44.95
	Understanding Everyday Australian - Book One	978 0 958539 50 0	$29.95
	Understanding Everyday Australian - Audio CD One (1)	978 1 877074 01 1	$19.95
	Understanding Everyday Australian - Teacher's Book One	978 0 958539 52 4	$44.95
	Understanding Everyday Australian - Book One & Audio CD	**978 1 877074 16 5**	**$39.95**
	Understanding Everyday Australian - Book Two	978 0 958539 53 1	$29.95
	Understanding Everyday Australian - Audio CD Two (1)	978 1 877074 02 8	$19.95
	Understanding Everyday Australian - Teacher's Book Two	978 0 958539 55 5	$44.95
	Understanding Everyday Australian - Book Two & Audio CD Pack	**978 1 877074 17 2**	**$39.95**
	Understanding Everyday Australian - Book Three	978 1 877074 20 2	$29.95
	Understanding Everyday Australian - Audio CD Three	978 1 877074 21 9	$19.95
	Understanding Everyday Australian - Teacher's Book Three	978 1 877074 22 6	$44.95
	Understanding Everyday Australian - Book Three & Audio CD	**978 1 877074 23 3**	**$39.95**
Beginner English	Word Building Activities for Beginners of English	978 1 877074 28 8	$29.95
	English Language Skills - Level One Student's Workbook	978 1 877074 29 5	$19.95
	English Language Skills - Level One Audio CD	978 1 877074 31 8	$19.95
	English Language Skills - Level One Teacher's Book	978 1 877074 32 5	$49.95
	English Language Skills - Level 1 Teacher's Book & Audio CD	978 1 877074 33 2	$59.95
Pronunciation & Spelling	Rhyming Stories - practice with the sounds and spelling of English (A5)	978 1 877074 06 6	$19.95
	Rhyming Stories -audio CD	978 1 877074 37 0	$19.95
	Rhyming Stories - language workbook (A4)	978 1 877074 38 7	$29.95
	Spelling and Pronunciation for English Language Learners	978 1 877074 04 2	$19.95
	Understanding English Pronunciation - Student book only	978 0 958539 57 9	$29.95
	Understanding English Pronunciation - Audio CD (Set of 3)	978 1 877074 03 5	$39.95
	Understanding English Pronunciation - Teacher's Book	978 0 958539 59 3	$44.95
Focus on 'International English'	Understanding Spoken English - Book One	978 1 877074 08 0	$29.95
	Understanding Spoken English - Audio CD One (1)	978 1 877074 10 3	$19.95
	Understanding Spoken English - Teacher's Book One	978 1 877074 11 0	$44.95
	Understanding Spoken English - Book One & Audio CD	**978 1 877074 18 9**	**$39.95**
	Understanding Spoken English - Book Two	978 1 877074 12 7	$29.95
	Understanding Spoken English - Audio CD Two (1)	978 1 877074 14 1	$19.95
	Understanding Spoken English - Teacher's Book Two	978 1 877074 15 8	$44.95
	Understanding Spoken English - Book Two & Audio CD	**978 1 877074 19 6**	**$39.95**
	Understanding Spoken English - Book Three	978 1 877074 24 0	$29.95
	Understanding Spoken English - Audio CD Three	978 1 877074 25 7	$19.95
	Understanding Spoken English - Teacher's Book Three	978 1 877074 26 4	$44.95
	Understanding Spoken English - Book Three & Audio CD	**978 1 877074 27 1**	**$39.95**

'Across Great Divides: True stories of life at Sydney Cove'

is a non-fiction narrative which brings to life the experiences of convicts aboard the First Fleet. The stories show varied responses to their unique situation in Australia's first colony.

The stories also give voice to the dilemma of the Aboriginal people challenged by the unexpected arrival of a completely alien race of white people to their land.

Yet meetings between the cultures would be dynamic and varied. The mystery of a new world had begun and the lives of all involved would never be the same again.

***

Susan is available for library and school visits to talk about the stories in her book.

See links to the Australian curriculum at www.birrong books.com

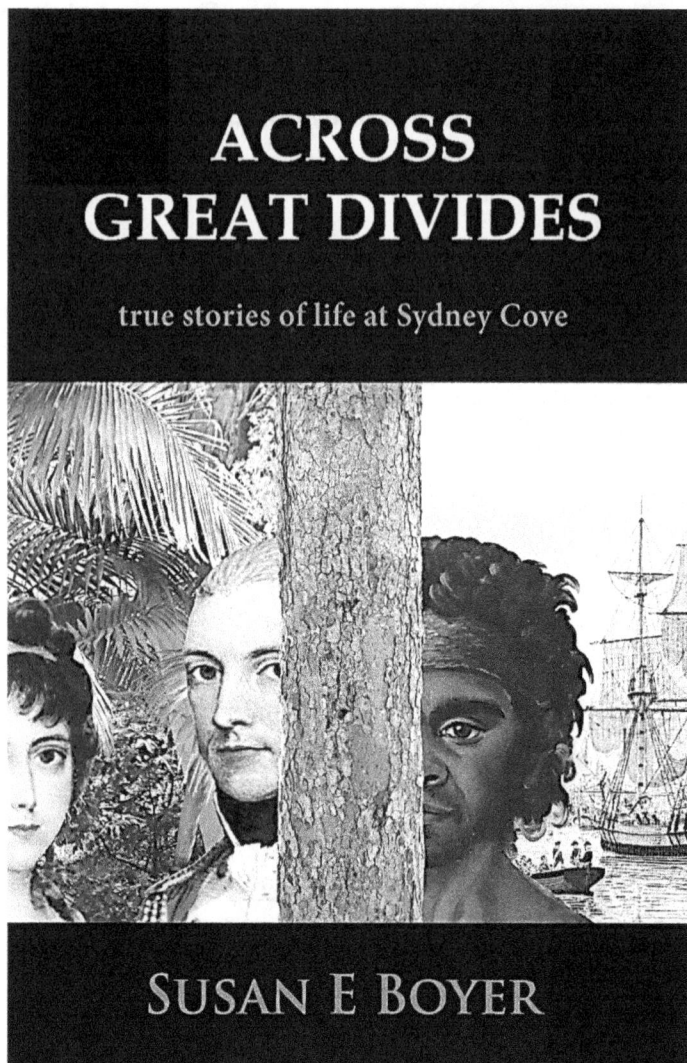

ACROSS GREAT DIVIDES

true stories of life at Sydney Cove

SUSAN E BOYER

A teacher's feedback following Susan's author talk at Windsor Library, NSW (where school students attended)

Hi Susan,
Our kids loved it. They were very engaged and came out saying they wanted more, which was just how my colleague and I felt! Their understanding was clear and I don't think you need to change anything for this level at school.
I was very proud of how involved and interested they were. Let us know if you do any more please!
Regards,
Julie Tuck, Year 5/6 teacher, Windsor Public School, NSW, September 2014

***

A reader's feedback following an author talk at Blaxland Library, NSW, May 2014.

Dear Susan,
I thoroughly enjoyed the book, I loved the way it was written and particularly liked that there were enough characters, but it was always easy to keep track of them. Another comment is the easy style of writing you have used. As I said I thoroughly enjoyed the book and I look forward to a future one.
Best regards,
Lachlan

'Across Great Divides: True Stories of Life at Sydney Cove'

Non-fiction Australian history - RRP $26.95

Available at bookstores across Australia or online at

www.birrongbooks.com

Free teaching resources and activities available at the above website

www.ingramcontent.com/pod-product-compliance
Lightning Source LLC
Chambersburg PA
CBHW081136090426
42742CB00015BA/2861
* 9 7 8 0 9 5 8 5 3 9 5 3 1 *